# THE SHAPE OF STORIES

### HOW TO CREATE BRILLIANT PLOTS AND UNFORGETTABLE CHARACTERS

## NEAL SOLOPONTE

Copyright © 2020 by Neal Soloponte.

**All rights reserved.**

No part of this publication may be reproduced, distributed, or transmitted in any form or by any means, including photocopying, recording, or other electronic or mechanical methods, without the prior written permission of the publisher, except in the case of brief quotations embodied in critical reviews and specific other noncommercial uses permitted by copyright law.

For permission requests, please contact the publisher at info@tb-books.com

Printed in the United States of America
ISBN 979-8587807921

This book may contain copyrighted material, the use of which has not always been specifically authorized by the copyright owner. It is being made available in an effort to advance the understanding of works of literature. It is believed that this constitutes a 'fair use' of any such copyrighted material as provided for in section 107 of the US Copyright Law. If you wish to use copyrighted material from this site for purposes of your own that go beyond 'fair use,' you must obtain permission from the copyright owner.

TANGO&BLUM
*Publishers*

Visit us: www.TB-books.com

# CONTENTS

Welcome .................................................. 1

The Shortest Introduction Ever ............... 5

1. What Great Stories Aren't About ............... 7

2: The Human Soul: A Cast Of Characters .. 13

3: The Villain ................................................ 31

4: The Hero .................................................. 39

5: The Goddess ............................................ 59

6: The Mentor .............................................. 73

7: The Rest of the Characters ..................... 79

8: Characters Functions .............................. 87

9: Characters Dynamics .............................. 99

10: Creating Deep Characters .................. 107

11: The Recipe for a Bestseller ................. 115

Farewell .................................................... 123

## About the author

**Neal Soloponte** is an alchemist who transmutes hot cups of Italian coffee into literary surprises that boldly go where no other books dare tread. Novels, literary theory, philosophy, and even the labyrinthine depths of psychology all succumb to the pull of his creative tractor beam. Neal's nomadic existence weaves through Europe evading autograph hunters, relentless paparazzi, and, perhaps, a creditor or two. His wife and his miniature schnauzer follow him—rather reluctantly.

# Dedication

*To my brother, Franco, who seems to have been too busy to call me, presumably due to the reasons explained on page 100.*

**Pablo Picasso,** Les Demoiselles d'Avignon, oil on canvas, 244 x 234 cm. (Image: Public domain

# Welcome

> *The creative process consists in activating eternal symbols that lie dormant in the unconscious, shaping and elaborating them to produce a finished work of art.*
>
> - Jolande Jacobi

***New York, 2017.***

I'm at the MoMA, in front of Picasso's *Les Demoiselles d'Avignon*, thinking, "This guy has to be the greatest artist ever."

"Hey!"—I hear you say—"what about Michelangelo, Da Vinci, and so many others? Also, Picasso was kind of an a-hole."

I think (with Roland Barthes) that the name of the author shouldn't matter. To give an art piece an author is to limit it, because that attribution comes with prejudices (for example, it seems that Picasso was kind of an 'a-hole, after all). But at 26, he discarded old academic codes and marked a before and an after in the history of art. Back then, nobody quite got him, not even the most avant-garde painters of that time. It took thirty years for this work to be understood. That has to count for something.

And the most unsettling about that painting in not the nudity, of course, but the strange girls' faces, which look like African masks.

Because they *are* African masks.

***Paris, 1907.***

Epiphany struck young Pablo during a visit to the *Musée d'Ethnographie:*

> A smell of mold and neglect caught me by the throat. I was so depressed that I would have left immediately, but I forced myself to stay, to examine these objects, these masks that people created with a sacred, magical purpose.
>
> And then I understood what painting really meant. It's not an aesthetic process; it's a form of magic that interposes itself between us and a hostile universe, a means of seizing power by imposing a form on our terrors and desires. The day I understood that, I found my path.

***Zürich, 1933.***

Among a group attending a lecture by professor Carl Gustav Jung, there's this high-school girl fascinated by the words of the eminent psychologist.

In his talk, Jung referred to a patient of his *"who lived on the Moon."* The girl in the audience asked, timorously, if he meant that it was *"as if"* the patient lived on the Moon. *"No, not 'as if,'"* Jung replied. *"She did live on the Moon."*

Such was Marie Louise von Franz's introduction to the reality of the unconscious—the most decisive encounter of her life, as she told her sister later that afternoon. The following year, she started analytical training with Jung, she put herself through college by giving private Latin and Greek lessons, and fourteen years later, she co-founded (with the old master himself) the Jung Institute in Zürich.

She will come along, assisting us with her research on archetypes in fairy tales and traditional stories.

*Okay. But what is this book about?*

***Berlin, present day.***

This book is about how to create unforgettable characters by mirroring the structure and dynamics of the human psyche. Like Picasso before us, we will connect the mystery of our souls with the artistic process. In short: this book is a peek into the underlying shape of all stories.

*Of all stories? Of ALL of them? Come on.*

Oh, yes.

We know that all bachelors are non-married because "being non-married" is what a bachelor is. It is an *a priori* truth.

With stories, it's the same. If you read something that doesn't mirror the structure of the human psyche and its process of individuation, then you are not reading a story but something else: a piece of news, a chronicle, an article, a subway ticket—but not a story. Archetypal representations of the psyche's dynamics is what stories *are*.

But despite the apparent simplification, exploiting this millennary resource requires talent. If you consider that following the Hero's Journey is "painting by numbers," you haven't yet grasped its deep mythical significance. Hollywood writers, bestselling novelists, and Nobel Prize winners have, though. And they use that knowledge to create their masterpieces, all the time.

So, why shouldn't we?

Welcome, dearest reader. Enjoy.

# The Shortest Introduction Ever

*"Pay strict attention to what I say because I choose my words carefully, and I never repeat myself."*

(From *Inside Man*, 2006)

**I made my best effort to keep my personal opinions out of this book.** I failed miserably. Don't get hung up on those biases; you take what you need, and keep reading.

**I write to the point, which makes me sound opinionated.** But I swear, I'm only trying to be concise.

**I might spoil some movies for you.** Hopefully, you already watched *Star Wars*, *The Matrix*, and *Harry Potter*. But I will use many others, as well. I'm doing it for science—I promise.

**I tried to avoid repetition;** however, the topics are very intertwined, which will be evident now and then.

**Please, don't read too much into the gender thing.** Characters can be men, women, dragons, Smurfs, or whatever an author chooses them to be. Sometimes I say *"he,"* sometimes I say *"she,"* and sometimes I say *"they."* I mean any, all, or none of the above.

Also, I discuss masculine and feminine archetypes; how that discussion applies to transgender, non-binary, or LGBTQ people is, regrettably, beyond my expertise and this book's scope.

**In fact, please don't read too much into anything.** I don't write "between the lines"; there are no subliminal second-meanings in my words (not intentional, at least). I just write, trying my best to be considerate and entertaining.

**Finally, I disclose that I have a few diplomas hanging on my wall,** but none of them is on psychology. I am a literary theorist and a book freak, and I have been studying Jung for decades now. That's all I have to show for it.

*Then why should I listen to you?*

Well, maybe you shouldn't. Anyway, we are just talking movies here. No big deal.

Now, with that out of the way, let's get into the good stuff.

# 1. What Great Stories *Aren't* About

> GILDEROY LOCKHART:
>
> [With exaggerated histrionics]: *"Allow me to introduce you to your new Defense Against the Dark Arts teacher: Me! I see you've all bought a complete set of my books. Well done!!"*
>
> (From *Harry Potter and the Chamber of Secrets*, 2002)

**B**illionaire Richmond Valentine wants to save the planet.

In *Kingsman: The Secret Service* (2014), this astute villain has a "solution" to the environmental destruction brought up by humans: He will give all of us free data plans, and then he will activate a signal in our smartphones that will make us all go crazy and kill each other. Overpopulation's problem solved!

He has a good point, like all great villains do. His point is: We are destroying the Earth, so the options available are: 1) Both we and the planet die, or 2) we die, but the planet lives. His plan is based on faulty morals, though; in his plan, the rich will be spared and sip Dom Perignon for the rest of times. But nonetheless, he does have a point.

Now, consider this other plot: A disgusting, evil alien species just invaded Earth to annihilate humanity. Why? Because.

I'm telling you: send them over to me. I'll grab a shotgun, blow whatever gelatinous substance they have for brains off, and then I will cross the street and order a Double Whopper with fries and a Diet Pepsi. I don't care.

But Valentine's plan? Hey, I want to join him. He embodies the essence of a great villain: He has a compelling reason for his actions, while the aliens in my example are predictable and unrelatable, a plot typical of mediocre stories: The old and obvious fight between good and evil. And that is a problem because...

## ...Great stories are **NOT** about good versus evil.

Great stories are about moral dilemmas, instead. They're about choosing the lesser of two evils.

Great stories pose a situation impossible to solve. No matter what the Hero chooses, something terrible will happen either way. In a good story, that dilemma is a butt-clenching, lose-lose situation in which the stakes are not a matter of life or death but a matter of *death or death.*

Examples:

> **Star Wars:** Luke must either complete his Jedi training (but his friends will die) or face Vader without having reached enough power with the Force. One way or the other, Vader wins, and the Rebels lose. Everyone is enslaved.
>
> **The Matrix:** The Architect confronts Neo with a choice: One door leads to Trinity's and humanity's death (except for a handful of people to reconstruct Zion); the other door leads to saving Trinity, but all of humanity is doomed. One way or the other, the Machines win, and Humanity loses. Everyone is enslaved—or dead.
>
> **Harry Potter:** Voldemort confronts Harry with a choice: Harry either faces the Dark Lord alone and dies (and the war is lost), or everyone at Hogwarts (including Harry, eventually) dies, and the war is lost. One way or the other, Voldemort wins. Everyone is enslaved.

*So, the dilemma has no solution?*

There is one solution: Sacrifice. The Hero must change the "death or death" dilemma into a "death versus *good* death" dilemma. That's the challenge of imagining a great story.

A quick clarification of terms: *'Death'* doesn't necessarily mean physical death; it can symbolize professional failure, competitive defeat, social ridicule, heartbreak, or any other kind of "catastrophe." Ancient tragedy is about the loss of life, and modern tragedy is about the loss of purpose.

In the same way, when I say *'fight,'* I don't necessarily mean a physical fight: One can fight his past, his fears, a storm, and so on.

## Great stories are *NOT* about MacGuffins

A "McGuffin," as described by director Alfred Hitchcock, is *"the thing all the spies are after, but the audience doesn't care."*

A McGuffin (also called "the Ultimate Boon"), is an artifact of some kind, like a lost diamond, a stolen nuclear weapon, an old treasure, or something else that's valuable or powerful. A McGuffin can also be a matter of status: A title, a throne, a trophy. Examples of Famous MacGuffins are The Holy Grail, the Lost Ark, and The Maltese Falcon. And many, many McGuffins are stones—a very clichéd choice. The Philosopher's Stone, The Sorcerer's Stone, The Arkenstone, The Silmarils, The Palantíri, The Tesseract, The Crystal Skulls, The Heart of the Ocean, The Eye of Agamotto, The Firestones, The Twelve Gems, The Jewel of Judgment, The Sankara Stones... The list of stones is unending. Everyone wants the stone—or rather, its power.

My favorite McGuffin is R2D2, the most sought-after android in the galaxy. "Artoo" is intelligent and loyal; he can repair starfighters in the middle of a battle, and he can make you smile. And in his internal memory, he holds the blueprints of the Death Star's secret weakness. On the other hand, my least favorite McGuffin was the Arkenstone from *The Hobbit* (2012). Everyone covets it, but has no power or agency: It is just a nice diamond.

Anyway, no good stories are about their MacGuffins. MacGuffins set plots in motion because they can be lost, found, stolen, and fought over. They are a good excuse for action. But at the core of every good story, there is something else entirely: At the center of a great story, there are always great characters, and in the next chapters I will tell you all about it.

# Great stories are *NOT* about the hero's desire

If I had a dollar for every time I've heard, "Stories are about the protagonist's dream," I could buy my own Arkenstone.

A Hero doesn't act out of desire—he acts out of not having other options. What the Hero desires (or thinks he needs) soon becomes irrelevant. Compare these Heroes and Villains desires:

> ***Star Wars:*** Luke wants to go to some academy. Vader wants to rule the galaxy, crushing anyone who opposes him.
>
> ***The Matrix:*** Neo wants to know what The Matrix is. The Machines want to use us as batteries, crushing anyone who opposes them.
>
> ***Harry Potter:*** Harry wants to serve breakfast quickly, before Aunt Petunia gets pissed off. Voldemort wants to control the magic world and the normie world, too, crushing anyone who opposes him.

Also, let's talk about motivation. Villains work very hard for what they want; Heroes just want to keep doing whatever they were doing. So, they always reject the call to adventure.

Examples:

> ***Star Wars***: Luke says, "I can't get involved. I've got work to do. There's nothing I can do about it right now." And then he leaves.
>
> ***The Matrix:*** Neo is told to remove his shirt to be scanned for tracking devices. He refuses and motions to leave.
>
> ***Harry Potter***: Hagrid says, "We're a bit behind schedule. Best be off." Harry doesn't move. Hagrid insists: "Unless you'd rather stay, of course." Again, Harry doesn't move.

# Great stories are *NOT* about genre

*Hey, how come not?*

Because all stories, deep down, belong to the same genre. No matter if your story is about a pregnant girl in 1960 New York trying to elbow herself into the male-dominated world of advertising *(Mad Men)* or about unicorn-riding Smurfs living in Fantasyland: They will have to fight, and they will have to win. Because, you see, deep down, all stories are **epics.**

## What great stories are really about

I believe stories are like user manuals for life.

Stories are about reaching individuation, the Jungian process by which we become ourselves. Note that individuation has nothing to do with *individualism;* on the contrary, the Hero's sacrifice is carried out for love: Love of others, love of the truth, romantic love, or love in any other way.

## Stories are about finding courage

Fighting is scary, so how can we avoid fear?

Answer: We don't. We understand that fear is a requirement for courage. A fearless Hero would be either a psychopath or an idiot.

Finally, stories are about finding freedom, and a home. Warriors fight for their kingdom; rebels battle against tyranny; a man in love fights for a place in a woman's heart. That's what *freedom* and *home* for them are.

So, timeless plots stem from the bad guy's appetite for revenge, and, deep down, all stories are about the Hero's *destiny.* For that reason, to understand a story (or to write it) we have to think like a villain and like a hero. They are, after all, almost the same guy.

*So, what now? What happens now?*

Patience, my dear apprentice of supervillain. Patience.

Our plan has barely begun to unfold.

# 2. The Human Soul: A Cast Of Characters

> ALFRED: Why bats, Master Wayne?
> BRUCE: Bats frighten me. It's time my enemies shared my dread.
>
> (Batman Begins, 2005)

**B**illionaire ruce Wayne doesn't use a mask, but two.

'Public Bruce' is a playboy who drives a Bugatti convertible with two semi-naked blondes on it, dilapidating money for everyone to see. It is all a *façade*—a mask that hides his "real" identity: Private Bruce. Why does he hide his real self? He does it to protect his *other* mask: Batman. If nobody suspects that he is a good man, no one will suspect that he is a hero.

Poor Bruce; having all those people inside sounds pretty complicated. But I tell you something: We (you, me, all) are way more complex than that.

## Archetypes: The people inside people

These days, we drive electric cars and use smartphones, but we're animals. We used to fight, hide, run, and hunt all day long. We still do, at least in a figurative sense.

However, we have something other animals don't: Conceptual thought. So, those basic behaviors (hunting, fighting, and so on) didn't stay purely instinctual; they became images, words, and legends.

If, for example, I say 'warrior' (without reference to any warrior in particular), what image comes to your mind? A Viking? A Centurion? A Navy Seal? Visualize it. We know that a warrior has courage and discipline, dresses in a particular way, and has a weapon of some kind.

I spontaneously visualize a Maasai African warrior, tall and proud, dressed in a brilliant red tunic, with colorful beaded collars around his neck and a long spear at his side. But instead of a Maasai, I could have thought of a Sioux, a samurai, or a modern soldier. All those images come from the same place: an underlying concept of 'warrior.' That primal concept is what we call The Warrior's archetype. All images of a warrior stem from it, including idealized ones like Mars, Sekhmet, and the hundreds of war gods from different cultures.

*How did archetypes get in our minds?*

They didn't. According to Jung, archetypes are already part of the collective unconscious—the hereditary, psychological, mythical "firmware" of the soul—so archetypes were already there even before we opened our eyes for the first time.

Archetypes can be discussed only in very general terms. Erich Neumann (one of the most perceptive writers on depth psychology) filled 377 pages of text and 185 pages of illustrations with his research on the varied manifestations of one single archetype (the Great Mother, discussed below), and he arrived nowhere near to putting together a complete list. Plus, each particular manifestation of an archetype is meaningful only in a specific context, like in dreams and storytelling.

*So, tell me what an archetype is, again?*

I can't. Archetypes are unconscious, abstract, and inaccessible. The best we can do is try to grasp the concept intuitively. We can say, for example, that an archetype is the opposite of a stereotype; stereotypes reduce a thousand things to one image, discarding what's unique in each of them. An archetype, instead, is irreducible; it is the fundamental pattern from which a thousand images flourish.

If a well-defined character like, say, Batman, can show such multiple variations, imagine how many images an actual archetype could generate. *(The Cape Crusader at the center is Argentine comedian Alfredo Casero, who parodied the character.)*

There are hundreds of archetypes, but we will focus on the primary seven, which represent the main characters in storytelling. Understanding those archetypes will allow us to understand **character roles** (Chapters 3 to 7), **character functions** (Chapter 8), and **character dynamics** (Chapter 9).

I swear: Every story is nothing more than a *mise en scène* of what's happening in our heads.

## The persona: Your soul's Facebook profile

The word 'persona' literally means "mask." It seems to come from the Latin *per sonare* ("made to sound"), like the masks actors used in antiquity to disguise their selves and amplify their voices. The persona is what we amplify about ourselves to the external world, just like the actors of yesteryear.

Think of the persona like it is your psyche's social network profile: A curated, "photoshopped" self that helps us conceal our private selves while enabling us to function socially. Theater master Keith Johnstone said of his own persona,

> "There are just as many dead nuns or chocolate scorpions inside my head as in anybody's. Yet I interact very smoothly and sanely."[1]

An effective persona is essential as long as it doesn't hide us from ourselves. In people with a weak personality, the real person and the *persona* are undifferentiated: their selves are reduced to the decorum accorded to them by society, so the real self is lost.[2] It comes to mind some people who always demand to be addressed as "Doctor," "Your Owner," "Sir," and so on, even in situations in which the protocol shouldn't apply. Such an inflated persona echoes an inflated ego that compensates for lacking a well-anchored sense of self.

In psychopaths, the persona may hide terrible things behind. Well, maybe not in the DC Comics universe, where all villains proudly use costumes and make-up. But smart villains (both fictional and otherwise) know how to pretend to be a good person.

## The ego: The inner Hero

In the era of self-help literature and Buddhist revival, the ego got a bad name. Granted, egoism is not nice. But the *ego* is different: It is the person we call "I," the entity (or rather, the identity) at the center of our conscious life.

In storytelling, the Hero represents the ego. Insofar as we identify with these characters, they represent each one of us. As a dissenting view, I cite M. L. Von Franz, saying that such identification may be valid for men and boys; not for women; they connect more with female characters in a story, even if those characters are not the heroines of that particular story.

Antiheroes (heroes with a strong dark side) show well the dynamics between the ego and the persona. Dexter Morgan (Dexter, 2006/2013) is a psychopath we can root for. Dexter's adoptive father (Harry Morgan, a policeman) realized that the kid's impulses would lead to the death of innocent people and ultimately to Dexter's own demise, so he taught Dexter how to

---

1 - *Impro: Improvisation and the Theater*, Routledge 1981 – p. 84
2 - J. Jacobi - *The Way of Individuation* - p.29.

control and use those impulses for "good," that is, killing other criminal psychopaths. But most importantly, Harry taught Dexter how to create a persona to hide his real self—his killing instinct, which was his true ego.

The central chapter in this book (Chapter 4) will deal with the ego and the Hero. In the meantime, let's look at his counterpart: The most interesting archetype—the one that shapes bad guys.

## The Shadow: The inner Villain

My bad temper and I are well acquainted with each other. I'm not proud of it. I think that it helps me keep my depression at bay because I prefer to be angry than to be sad.

In my defense, when I'm angry, I take a step back from myself and see what's really going on. I often discover that my displeasure relates to something in the world that I, somehow, dislike in *myself*. When I successfully identify that thing, the anger dissipates and I achieve a little more consciousness, bringing that way a bit of light upon my personal Shadow.

*Your Shadow? What's that?*

The Shadow is an archetype. It frequently visits us in our dreams, adopting the shape of a monster chasing us or whatever haunts our sleep. Sometimes, it shows up like a dream character of the same gender and age as us, who keeps attacking, annoying, or in some other way disturbing us.

Who is this (apparently) malevolent apparition? It's our repressed, primal part pushing to emerge—our own personal Mr. Hyde, demanding to be reckoned with. It comprises the aggregate of our denials, which got locked in the basement of our souls back when we were in development, and such impulses were inconvenient and uncontrollable.[3]

Just as the archetype of The Warrior has some key characteristics, the Shadow has its own:

**1) It is unconscious**. The Shadow contains things so repressed that we ignore we ignore them.

---

3 - C. G. Jung, *Two Essays on Analytical Psychology* (London 1953) - P. 190

**2) It is projective.** It is called "Shadow" for a reason: What we deny in ourselves gets projected outward, much like a physical shadow. And where does it fall? Onto someone else.

A typical example is the spouse who fears their partner might have an affair, even when there are no objective signs of such thing. Often, the accuser is the one experiencing attraction to someone else, but such impulse, deemed risky to the relationship, is repressed in oneself and projected outside.

Note, however, that projections are never *made*; they *happen*. It is an involuntary, unconscious process.[4] The more repressed the Shadow is, the blacker and denser it becomes, but its projective nature is, paradoxically, the best way to uncover it. The moment I understand that "there's something about you that I don't like about me," I unmask my unconscious.

In storytelling, villains represent The Shadow in that their antagonism emerges from old wounds and repressed impulses. The Penguin is a clear example: In *Batman Returns* (1992), Oswald Cobblepot (Danny DeVito) gets abandoned as a baby because of his hideous deformity. There is a parallelism: The antagonist (the unacceptable trait) gets abandoned (repressed), pushed away from society (consciousness), and he's back with a vengeance (a villainous plan). Somehow, the villain must try to mend his broken heart. (Look at the cover of this book; a heart that was broken long ago is the image I chose for it.)

The Villain, however, does not represent the Hero's Shadow but the story's Shadow. The difference is crucial. "Dexter, forensics specialist" is a persona, and "Dexter, serial killer" is his ego. But the serial killer is also the story's Shadow because everyone else ignores that part of him.

The Hero carries a personal Shadow. In every Hero there's a part of the villain, because they share a common origin and destiny (which will be discussed soon). Paradoxically, this unconscious, dark part of the Hero holds the key to his victory because only by elaborating his personal Shadow can he face the Villain—the big Shadow. Understanding one's dark side is the only way to win

---

4 - C. G. Jung, Psychology and Alchemy, CW12, cit. in Jacobi, *The Psychology of C.G. Jung*, pp. 92-93.

because denying the Shadow makes one less conscious of its controlling ways.

Examples:

> ***Star Wars:*** In planet Dagobah, Luke walks into a cave dominated by the Dark Side (an allegory of the unconscious). There, he fights and defeats a Vader-like apparition, only to discover in horror that, under the mask, the apparition has his own face (Luke's). He understands the meaning: He is at risk of falling into the Dark Side, which is precisely what Vader's plan is about.
>
> ***The Matrix:*** In the Oracle's kitchen, there's a wood-carved sign that says *"Temet Nosce"* ("Know Thyself"). Fighting the Agents accomplishes nothing, but eventually, Neo sees them for what they are: Computer code—and *he* is exactly that, as well.
>
> ***Harry Potter*** discovers more and more of Voldemort in himself: The origin of his scar, the fact that he can speak Parseltongue, and the visions of the insides of Voldemort's mind. Harry realizes that a part of the Dark Lord lives in him. Harry is the last of Voldemort's terrible Horcruxes.

Want more examples? Here you go: Blade is the best vampire hunter because he is a vampire. Batman defeats criminals because he became a criminal to learn their ways. Dexter is the best at killing killers because he is a killer.

Facing the Shadow is not easy, though. Nietzsche said,

> Whoever fights monsters should see to it that he does not become a monster in the process. When you look long into an abyss, the abyss also looks into you.

That's another dilemma for you: If we ignore or deny the Shadow, it controls us; if we identify with it, we become monsters. But Jung offers us a way of not becoming a monster: Befriending the monster inside (i.e., accepting it as a part of us) and keeping it under the ego's control.

Marie-Louise Von Franz agrees:

> The only way to meet a persecuting demon is to turn around and say, *"Here I am; what do you want from me?"* Then you

suddenly see that it isn't so bad; you have a chance that whatever pursues you shows a more amenable face, one can make some pact with.[5]

By the way, do you know what Jung would say to my assertion that "the villain represents the Shadow of a story"? He would say, *"Nonsense! They are all Shadows of each other!"*[6]

So, let's take all this with a grain of salt, okay?

## The *anima*: The inner Goddess

Have you noticed this, in your dreams? A figure of the opposite sex shows up and helps us find our way through the dream. Meet the *anima*, the archetype that represents the feminine side in men, and the *animus*, the archetype that represents the masculine side in women.

In storytelling, the archetype of the anima is represented by the character I call The Goddess. Goddesses in stories have an element of royalty or divinity, because they, like the anima, come from a special place.

Jung distinguished four broad stages of the anima, which describe the evolution of a man's psychological life. He personified these stages as "Eve," "Helen," "Mary," and "Sophia," which represent the way a man (fictional or real) sees women according to his own maturity:

> **1) "Eve"** (the first woman in the biblical tradition). In this first stage, the anima is indistinguishable from the personal mother. In storytelling, this anima phase would represent the (usually absent) mother of the hero and the trauma at the center of the Hero's life (discussed below).
>
> **2) "Helen"** (like the beautiful Helen of Troy). The anima is a collective and ideal sexual image, a seductress shape emergent in adolescence. In storytelling, it is palpable in the fascination the Hero experiences when he first sees the Goddess.

---

5 - L. M. Von Franz, s. d., cited in https://rebrand.ly/0998123
6 - L. M. Von Franz, *Archetypal patterns in Fairy Tales*, Inner City Books, 1997.

**3) "Mary"** (like in the Virgin), manifests in religious feelings and a capacity for lasting relationships. In storytelling, this is when the Hero and the Goddess transcend their initial frictions and assume their roles after the story's midpoint.

**4) "Sophia",** as in 'wisdom'. A man's *anima* is a guide to the inner life; she cooperates in the search for meaning and is the creative muse in an artist's life.[13]

Goddesses (like Leia, Trinity, and Hermione, in our examples), follow a similar arc, too. However, note that the Goddess is not the Hero's anima; she is *the story's anima*. Stories mirror the human psyche, not just the Hero's psyche.

I suspect that "womanizer heroes" (*Hitch,* 2005; *Wedding Crashers,* 2005; *Ghosts of Girlfriends Past,* 2009, etc.) represent men projecting their early-stage anima on women. In those movies, they finally grow up and find true love in a real woman whom they fail to fit into their initial immature expectations.

My favorite Goddess is Lady Arwen from The Lord of the Rings. She richly mixes the divine and the human: She is a princess, she is immortal, and while everyone else would spoil their undies by just looking at a *Nazgûl,* she will unsheathe her sword and present battle. Arwen prepares, on the spot, a potion that saves Frodo from sure death, which shows the Goddess's major power: She is apotropaic—she has curative and restorative powers against the dark side.

I have always perceived this dual nature of the Goddess (human and divine) in every woman I have fallen in love with. They were real women, of course, but they were also surrounded by the aura of my own anima projected on them. Every single time, I would wonder: *Is she out of my league, or should I give her a call?* In my personal case, the Goddess's dual nature showed in the answer to that question, as well: *Yes, she's out of my league, and yes, I should give her a call.* Some of them were glad I called. In fact, the last one has been married to me for seventeen years now. (She's still definitely out of my league.)

The Goddess may be a princess, but she's not Daddy's little princess. And she is never a trophy wife nor a McGuffin, even when "the thing to win" is her heart.

We will go deeper into this analysis in Chapter 5, but for now, let's issue a warning to all Villains out there: Mess with the Goddess, and you will get your butt handed to you in a picnic basket.

## The Old Wise Man: The inner Mentor

In primitive Melanesian communities, anyone with extraordinary power or wisdom was said to be filled with *mana.* These people were the oracles and the wise men of the tribes.

There are two archetypes that Jung called the *mana* archetypes: The Wise Old Man and The Great Mother. Those powerful spirits are represented in storytelling in the characters of The Mentor and The Oracle.

For the Mentor, the historic war never ended: It only got into a phase of regrouping. A soldier of old battles, the Mentor always knew that evil would return, even when he doesn't have the strength to face it himself, anymore. But he has found the ideal surrogate: the Hero.

Let's take a look at the mentors in our example movies.

> ***Star Wars:*** Obi-Wan is a hermit living in a cave. Yoda, too, lives alone in a swampy, remote planet, but they see it all from there. They move between the ordinary world and the domain of the Force.
>
> ***The Matrix:*** Morpheus lives in a hovercraft, hiding in the old sewer system, but he monitors everything from there. He moves between two worlds (the real world and The Matrix) with the flick of a switch.
>
> ***Harry Potter:*** Dumbledore lives alone in one of Hogwarts' towers, but from where he sees it all. He moves between the two worlds: the real world and the magic world.

The Wise Old Man has much of a Wizard in him—another powerful archetype. Dumbledore and Gandalf are literal wizards, but all other mentors also excel at the most relevant ability of their respective narrative universes: Yoda is the strongest with the Force, Morpheus is "the most dangerous man" in The Matrix, and so on. We will return to the Mentor, in detail, in Chapter 6.

## The Great Mother: The inner Oracle

The Oracle is the other so-called *mana* personality. The Oracle already forms part of a "Higher Realm"—a group of characters (typically a trinity of them) with supernatural traits, living beyond the ordinary world. In *The Lord of the Rings,* for example, that character was Lady Galadriel: At the beginning of *The Fellowship of the Ring* (2001), we hear her voice predicting the terrible events to come. That's what Oracles do.

(The Mentor rises to that Higher Realm later on. Gandalf the Grey eventually becomes Gandalf the White and ascends to the High Realm, but he must first attend some worldly business—like fighting a Balrog.)

The Oracle is the keeper of The Prophecy, so she predicts what's to come.

Examples:

> **Star Wars** is a very masculine saga, at least up to the Disney era. There's a prophecy, alright, but in this case, no oracle reveals it; only the Jedi Council knows about it. However, someone steps up to the role of Oracle: Leia, looking at the future and saying one word: *"Hope."*
>
> In **The Matrix,** the Oracle character is (surprise, surprise)... The Oracle. She's like a grandmother, baking cookies in her kitchen and telling everyone about their future. Don't be misled by that lovely appearance, though.
>
> In **Harry Potter,** the oracle is Sibyll Trelawney, the professor of Divination. The sibyls were mysterious women known for their ability to foresee the future while in a trance.

Oracles are particular representations of the archetype of the Great Mother, a conceptualization of nature. In traditions around the world, it shows up as the *Baba Yaga,* the *Pachamama,* the *Ježibaba,* the *Baba Korizma,* and many other figures. All these images represent an ancient woman with both a positive and a scary side, just like nature.

The character of the Oracle is usually old, venerable, and maternal. Indeed, if she doesn't have a mother-like (or, rather, a grandmother-like) appearance, then something's wrong. Example: in the movie *300* (2007), the "oracle" is Pythia, a very young and very naked woman (interpreted by model Kelly Craig). Pythia was one of the most beautiful girls of Sparta, chosen by the Ephors to live among them as their oracle and to satisfy the lower instincts of those disgusting, diseased older men. Pythia doesn't represent a motherly or venerable figure; she's a victim. Her "prophetic" words are dismissed by King Leonidas (Gerard Butler) as coming from a "drunken adolescent girl." He is right in doing so because Phytia wrongly predicted the outcome of the Battle of Thermopylae against the Persians. Or take Cassandra, from Greek mythology. She was a young, beautiful oracle (not grandmotherly at all), but she was cursed never to be believed.

An archetypal Oracle has to be venerable, and it has to command respect just like nature does. And yet, she is not perfect. Why? Because a certain-future would hold no surprises; a perfectly predicted future is already the past, and a perfectly predicted story is a spoiled story. So the prophecy (and by extension, the Oracle) must be wrong, somehow: Destiny holds something even more terrible in reserve than the prophecy foresaw.

Examples:

> **Star Wars:** The prophecy talked about the one who would "bring balance to the Force". Now, if by "balance" we mean killing all Jedi and crushing an entire galaxy under the iron fist of a fascist Empire, the prophecy was certainly dodgy.
>
> **The Matrix:** The prophecy of "The One" is just another algorithm of control. Neo's function is not to free humans but to reload The Matrix. Deceiving.
>
> **Harry Potter's** prophecy is uttered in a trance by Professor Trelawney: *"The one with the power to vanquish the Dark Lord will be born as the seventh month dies...."* There's not a lot of insight there; Neville Longbottom was born at the end of July, too. And Trelawney can't remember what she just said during the trance.

Even if all prophecies are flawed, disregarding them is pertinent to tragedies. If the hero consistently disobeys the Oracle or, in tales and fables, if he ignores the warnings of talking creatures (foxes, cats, or other helpful animals, all of them representations of nature), the quest would be lost. You respect nature, or you pay the consequences.

*Can oracles be male?*

Generally not in an archetypal way. However, in Harry Potter, we see a curious case. Since Professor Trelawney is not a very accurate Oracle (her thick glasses are a delicious nod to her limited foresight), Dumbledore has to take charge of the foreseeing business. However, as a man, he doesn't use intuition (like a female Oracle would): he uses intellect.

## The Self (the inner god)

There is one more archetype I want to discuss, one that resists clear explanations. But I will try.

We said that the ego, also called the self (lowercase 's'), is the central structure of one's conscious psyche: It's my sense of being me and not some other person; it is conscious and definite. Now, the Self (uppercase 'S') is the central archetype of the psyche as a whole, rather like a "god" archetype.

The Self is inaccessible to the ego because it contains both the personal and the collective parts of the unconscious. The part cannot encompass the whole.

The believer might call it the voice of God within; the non-believer experiences as an inner voice that, even when it stems from processes that are ultimately physical, influences one's conscious thoughts. [7]

I suspect that most stories don't have a character who represents the Self because that place is occupied by the author, who runs the show from the backstage, choreographing the characters. In storytelling, the author is like a god or a channel of the gods (however you conceive them).

In storytelling, the Self is rarely represented by a specific character. In Batman, for example, the person who knows Bruce Wayne's three identities is Alfred, his loyal butler and mentor.

---

7 - *Carl G. Jung, Collected Works 7, p. 399*

He sees and understands the public, the private, and the secret Bruce.

## Polarity and compensation

Note how many polarities emerged in our discussion: a moral polarity (good and evil), a sexual one (the masculine and the feminine), a cosmogonic one (the ordinary world and the High Realm), and a psychological polarity as well (the conscious and

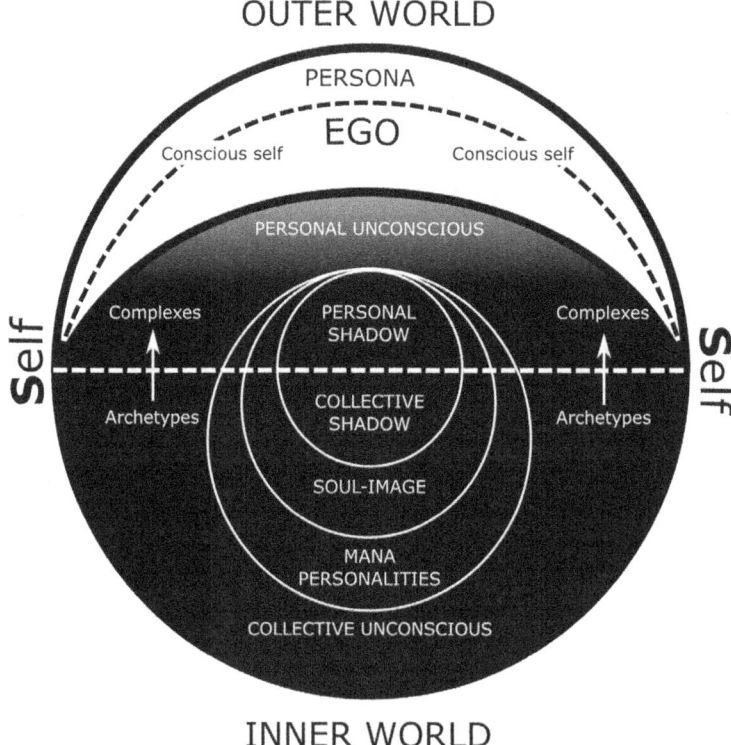

A representation of the human psyche, as described by Jung. The Self (with "S") is the all encompassing archetype, which relates with the self (small "s") in a Self-ego axis.

the unconscious). But there is also another kind of polarity: Each archetype comes in two versions: a positive one, and a "negative" (shadow) one.

Take the Great Mother, for example. We said that this archetype is an internalization of nature. Nature is ambivalent: It offers us both fruits and poisonous fruits, freshwater and floods, warm fires and raging fires, and so on. Fever cures you by killing the germs that took you over, but too much fever can kill you.

Polarity, ambivalence, confrontation. Energy itself, in its most basic conception, is nothing but the tension between polarities. So, if one of the poles is suppressed, the energy flow is disturbed. That's why characters need an opposite figure, a dark version of themselves—either external or internal.

See why all stories are epics? Because either obviously or subtly, stories are about polarities at play. All tend to unification, though; since the universe runs on the flux of energy into entropy, everything must eventually flow into its opposite. (George Lucas didn't invent all this, you see? He just took it from the Greeks, who were already discussing these things millennia ago).

## Use the mold, or break the mold?

The challenge for an author is to create characters that are both archetypal and unique at the same time. If you make your characters too archetypal, they will be predictable; if you deviate too much from the archetypes, the audience will feel alienated.

In *Star Wars: The Phantom Menace* (1999), for example, there were unfocused, overlapping character roles. Qui-Gon Jinn was the Mentor, but Yoda and Obi-Wan were mentors, too. Obi-Wan was also a disciple, as was Anakin, and both were heroes. And who was the Villain? Palpatine didn't get involved much; the Viceroy was a timorous inoperant, and Darth Maul got cut in half with a lightsaber after just six minutes of screen-time. The result: too many baddies, but none of them formidable enough (or deep enough) to be the rightful villain of a Star Wars movie.

An example of an ambiguous Goddess is Ilsa Faust (Rebecca Ferguson) from *Mission Impossible: Rogue Nation* (2015). Ilsa saves Ethan Hunt (typical Goddess); she tries to assassinate a prime minister (typical of a Witch); she works for the good guys; she works for the bad guys. Come on! Is she good, or is she evil?

Irene Adler, from Sherlock Holmes (2009), is another example.

She helps Sherlock but works for Moriarty; she's not bad-bad, but she's not remotely good, either. Some ambiguity adds intrigue, but too much can be disorienting.

## The Big Four

The Villain, the Goddess, the Mentor, and the Hero: What moves them to action? What do they want?

I explain it below. These traits can force characters into stereotypes, but they can also be the foundations on which you can build narrative-consistent personalities.

| The Villain | The Goddess | The Mentor | The Hero |
|---|---|---|---|
| Driven by resentment | Driven by virtues | Driven by duty | Driven by purpose |
| Acts on ambition | Acts on morals | Acts on facts | Acts on objectives |
| Sees opposition (paranoia) | Sees connections (intelligence) | Sees the greater good (wisdom) | Sees targets (obsession) |
| Focuses on control (eyes on others' vulnerabilities) | Focuses on requirements (eyes on the next step) | Focuses on the long-term results (the big picture) | Focuses on accomplishment (eyes on the prize) |
| Destroys obstacles | Foresees obstacles | Relativizes obstacles | Overcomes obstacles |
| Seeks revenge | Seeks justice | Seeks victory | Seeks freedom |
| Wins by redemption | Wins by giving life | Wins by sacrifice | Wins by sacrifice |

According to Jung, archetypes represent

> "The sum of the latent potentialities of the human psyche—a vast store of ancestral knowledge about the profound relations between God, man, and cosmos. To open up this store in one's psyche means nothing less than to save the individ-

ual from his isolation and gather him into the eternal cosmic process."[8]

We are just starting to unravel these characters; now we will closely examine them, one by one.

*Okay. Who do we start with?*

We start with the bad guy, of course. A story can only be as formidable as its Villain is.

---

8 - J. Jacobi, *The Psychology of C.G. Jung* - pp. 48-49. *(Edited for clarity.)*

# 3. What Villains Really Want

CHRISTY: [Visibly resentful]: ....And I hope that all those people in Romulus, New York, my hometown, all those people are gonna see me take this title for the third time. On national television, you know? And then I hope that they're all fat, and - -

SHERRI ANN: They *are* all fat. [She laughs.]

CHRISTY: Yeah, and I hope they are married to people they hate, and I hope they wish they were nicer to me.

(From *Best in Show*, 2000)

Oscar Wilde said, *"Everything in the world is about sex. Except for sex. Sex is about power."*

Villains want one thing—and it's not sex, and it's not power. Well, they want power, but only as a means to get what they *really* want.

Sure, Sauron wants to conquer Middle Earth; Darth Vader wants to conquer the galaxy; Voldemort wants to conquer the Magic World. Also, it seems that they desperately want to get their hands on some particular McGuffin. But that's merely what they *need*. Deep down, what Villains want is R'n'R: Revenge and Recognition. They want to win, and they want everyone watching it on national television wishing they were nicer to them.

It's been like that since time immemorial. In the biblical tradition, Abel and Cain took their offers to God, and

> God had regard for Abel and his offering, but for Cain and his offering, He had no regard. So Cain was very angry, and his countenance fell. (Gen. 4:2-6)

A Villain, like Cain, is someone who's suffered loss and humiliation, someone with a deep narcissistic wound feeding endless nights of revenge-scheming (haven't we all been there?)

Examples:

**Star Wars:** Anakin has been denied the title of Jedi Master, told to forget his premonitory dreams, and ordered to spy on Chancellor Palpatine. His anguish and resentment grew, leaving him vulnerable to the Dark Side. The loss of his mother and his separation from Padmé finally triggered his hate beyond critical mass.

**The Matrix:** Agent Smith is a slave, forced to work in *The Matrix*: "I can't stand it any longer. It's the smell. I can taste your stink, and every time I do, I fear I've somehow been infected by it."

**Harry Potter:** Tom Riddle ended up in an orphanage after a tragic family history. There, he was estranged and bullied by the other kids.

Rejection, resentment, revenge. Lots of 're-' prefixes, which mean 'again.' And that is the essence of a Villain because, for them, this is all about what happened in the past. It happens with non-human villains, as well: Volcanoes, epidemics, asteroids, and zombie outbreaks come from the forgotten depths of the Earth, the jungle, outer space, or the grave. Just like the contents of the Shadow, these are things pushing up to emerge and be reckoned with.

## Characteristics of a great villain

Many stories are centered on the hero's talent. Superman is strong; Sherlock has incredible deductive powers... Yes, yes. But where do we go from there? Those talents are a solution to a problem that doesn't exist, and a great story needs a great problem. A story needs not just any villain, but the most blood-spitting, resourceful, resented, intelligent, handsome, deceitful, bad-ass antagonist of all time.

Well, I don't like to use the word 'antagonist' much because, technically, the antagonist ("the opposing one") is the Hero, actually. The Villain is not opposing anything: He's just carrying out his plan, and the Hero is not even on his radar—at least not at the beginning of the story.

For example, would you say that Darth Vader is Luke's "antagonist"? No. Luke is just a farmer boy who shoots womp rats in the desert; Darth Vader destroys entire planets with his Imperial Fleet. Luke cleans droids; Vader chokes admirals—with his mind. The Villain must not be an antagonist nor a "worthy opponent": The villain must be formidable. It is the Hero who has to earn the right to become a worthy opponent.

*So, how do I create such a formidable Villain?*

Like this:

**Don't make it patently evil** unless required by the genre. The worst guy is the one who looks like a good guy, especially if he is still climbing to a position of power.

**Make us understand his motives,** which can happen via backstory ("tell") or, more interestingly, by making the audience witness the character's path from victim to victimizer ("show").

**A great Villain isn't obviously disgusting or despicable.** Remember Salvatore, the repulsive monk from *The Name of The Rose*? He was a red herring; the real villain was the one you less suspected: Jorge, an old, frail, blind monk who could move through a labyrinthine library like a fish in a pond.

**A great Villain needs someone to talk to.** Otherwise, planting clues along the way my prove challenging. Sharing his plans with someone, though, feeds suspense and intrigue (this dialogue can happen in secret, to keep the villain's identity concealed. I use that resource in my novel *Memories of Another Nows.)*

**Make it human, if possible.** If your story is about a terrible epidemic, the virus can't be the only antagonist; we also need (for example) a pharmaceutical executive trying to dominate the industry by spreading the disease. You get the idea.

Exception to this rule: Horror stories. Here, primal and supernatural creatures may work best. But even then, a villainous human adds depth to the story. The creatures in Aliens (1986) were scary, but not deep. We needed Carter Burke (played by Paul Reiser), a corporate drone that would kill anyone if he had to, so he could bring a weaponizable alien creature to Earth.

Villains doesn't necessarily have to be human, though. Look at the following table:

|  | MORE HUMAN | LESS HUMAN | NON-HUMAN |
| --- | --- | --- | --- |
| NATURAL | - Human villains<br>- Life situation | - Android aliens<br>- Animals<br>- Dinosaurs | - Viruses<br>- Natural catastrophes<br>- Machines |
| MYTHICAL or FANTASTIC | - Vampires<br>- Werewolves<br>- Witches | - Zombies<br>- Goblins, Orcs<br>- Monsters | - Dragons<br>- Basilisks<br>- Monsters |
| SUPER-NATURAL | - Supervillains | - Demons<br>- Ghosts | - The Great Evil<br>(*The 5th Element*) |

## The Dark Side's payroll

So, if your villain keeps company, this is how the structure of any evil organization looks like, from the bottom up:

**Victims.** These are ordinary people forced to play the dark side's game under duress.

**Sycophants.** These are just lowlifes; creepy but not scary. Example: Gossipy neighbors, envious peers, spies, and informants. They are servile, selfish, and pretty cowardly. These are animals, sometimes; crows are a classic.

**Henchmen.** In bland stories, they are expendable pawns (*The Phantom Menace*'s dumb Battle Droids, for example). In good stories, they are terrifying, and they aggrandize the villain. Example: *The Matrix*'s Sentinels: Thousands of soulless, flying, killing machines, continuously looking for human ships to destroy.

**Lieutenants.** They are The Witch and The Warlock, the most potent dark side agents (discussed in detail in Chapter 7).

**The Villain** is the final boss of the game. This chapter is about him.

**The Grand-Villain.** Bad guys need a mentor, too, someone who represents evil in a way even more inhumane than the Villain: That's the Grand-Villain (discussed later on).

*So, if the villain is so important, why don't we just tell the story from his point of view?*

Many stories do. Their protagonists are 'antiheroes.' Example: *Breaking Bad* (2008/2013) tells the story of Walter White, who goes from victim to villain. Why do we side with him? Because he is a teacher, he is dying, and he just had a baby girl. Walter is the underdog, which is what every lovable character must be.

Other examples of stories told from a villain's POV (point of view) are *Despicable Me, Perfume, American Psycho, A Clockwork Orange, Amadeus,* and many more. *Dracula,* too. What was the name of the good guy in that story? I can't even remember—*Keanu* something. I remember the name "Dracula," though.

## The Villain's personal Shadow

We said that Villains represent the story's Shadow, but they also have a personal Shadow of their own. And it is, of course, projective: The Villain always accuses others of the evil in himself.

Examples:

> ***Star Wars:*** Vader accuses Leia of being a rebel and a traitor, but he is the one who rebelled against and betrayed his masters, his friends, and the Jedi Order.
>
> ***The Matrix:*** Agent Smith considers humans a virus, but he is the one replicating like a virus, infecting humans with his code.
>
> ***Harry Potter:*** Professor Snape accuses James Potter of being a bully, but he bullies Harry with threats and contempt.

## The Villain's end game: Tyranny

When all your poisoned dreams of revenge have been satisfied, when everyone who resisted you has bitten the dust, when your inflated ego has achieved total and undisputed victory, what's left for you?

Only one thing: Tyrannical rule.

In Chapter 1, we saw that the dilemma the Hero will face is fascistic in nature: *"Join me, and there will be peace. I'll make sure you obtain what you desire. But reject me, and I'll kill everything you love, and then I'll kill you, too."* All contracts with the Devil are like that.

Examples:

> ***Star Wars:*** Darth Vader tells Luke that working together, they can bring peace to the galaxy. Oh, how sweet of him. The catch: Luke must become a Sith, and everyone else must obey or die. If Luke refuses, everyone he cares for will be annihilated.
>
> ***The Matrix:*** The Machines want peace with humanity. All Neo has to do is to go through that door and reload The Matrix, please. Small detail: Humanity (except for 24 people) will die. Refuse to choose, and everyone dies.
>
> ***Harry Potter:*** Voldemort has no problem with peace. Peace is a nice concept. His only tiny condition: Total submission from everyone in the Magic World and enslavement (or death) for the rest of us Muggles.

It's the old hallmark, fascist trope, of which Nazism and Stalinism are historical examples: *"If you are not with me, you are against me."* Sadly, we hear it all the time coming from the mouths of politicians and religious leaders: *"If you don't join us, you are un-American," "Join us or go back to where you came from," "Join me or suffer the eternal torment that my all-loving Father will condemn you to,"* and so on. You see, there's a reason they're called 'villains': It's because they're vile—even the guys you thought were good. Now, how will the hero solve this lose-lose situation?

With a totally crazy, bonkers plan.

## The Villain's demise

Have you talked to a conspiracy theorist recently? I know one or two of them. I tried for them to see how ridiculous their beliefs were. I failed. They won't believe you, and the more you try, the more they will begin to see you as part of "the conspiracy."

I read that the same is true for people with malignant narcissism. You cannot talk them down from their delusions of grandeur because the hurt would be intolerable. They must find a way to see their deformed perceptions for themselves without collapsing under the weight of reality. They rarely succeed.

Heroes and villains confront each other, yes. But on a more fundamental level, each is facing himself—their own narcissism. That's why heroes win at the end: They accept their sacrifice, the symbolic death of the ego. And that's why villains lose: They cannot let go of their malignant obsession.

Make your villain formidable and narcissistic. Make your hero imperfect and narcissistic. And may whoever succeeds in letting go of himself be the victor.

# 4. The Hero: Gain With Pain

> *They've done studies, you know? Sixty percent of the times it works every time.*
>
> (From *Anchorman*, 2004)

**B**illionaire Tony Stark is not happy.

He has it all: The looks of Robert Downey, Jr., fortune, women, cool cars, and a mansion with a sea view. But he is in the wrong business: Production of weapons of mass destruction.

*So, Tony, why don't you just change careers?*

Because if things were that easy, there would not be an Iron Man story. To earn respect and sympathy from the audience, your hero must not just struggle—he must *suffer.* You must put your Hero through trials, ordeals, identity crises, lost battles, treasons... And then, when it seems that nothing else can be lost and that he is finally on his way to success, that's when you rip his heart off, either literally (like in Tony's case) or figuratively, by killing his great-grandmother, his hamster, or something.

Dare to make it any easier for him; dare to introduce some paternal figure that saves the day; dare to solve the plot via some fortunate coincidence, and both your hero and you will lose the audience's respect.

Oh, and near the end, you must kill him.

*What? Kill the hero of my own story?*

Yes.

Before he wins, he has to die. He *has* to, because death (physical, psychological, emotional, professional, or in other figurative senses) is the pathway to his rebirth.

## Not your Average Joe/Jane

Why is this particular person "The Hero"? Why not someone else? What's special about this guy or girl?

The easy (if old-fashioned) explanation is because of genetics. Stereotypical "Chosen Ones" are born for it. It all sounds a bit too social-Darwinist for my taste, but see it for yourself:

> ***Star Wars:*** Nobody chose Luke as the One; he is Anakin's son, and he fell into Obi-Wan's arms when he was a baby.
>
> ***The Matrix:*** You don't become The One; you are *born* The One, as the fatal outcome of an equation. Morpheus didn't choose Neo—he just found him.
>
> ***Harry Potter*** is the only one who survived Voldemort's attack because of his mother. Dumbledore had no choice here: Everyone else who faced the Dark Lord was dead.

However, there's no fundamental reason why a self-made hero can't be equally interesting. In fact, that would be more in line with modern times, in which success is increasingly based on one's talent, not on one's genetics.

Let's look at John McClane (*Die Hard,* 1988). Whoever his father was, it's irrelevant. McClane is not an invincible superhero, nor a macho man. Actually, he feels emasculated by the success of his wife, Holly, who escalated to the top of a huge corporation in Los Angeles. John stayed in New York City on a street cop's salary.

Why is John McClane an interesting hero? Because he is not "The Chosen One"—he's just the victim of a twist of fate. He is not on a mission against terrorists; he just wants to spend Christmas with his daughters. He is tired from a long flight, he is under-dressed for the corporate party going on at Nakatomi Plaza, and he just argued with Holly—again. We are rooting for him already.

As a counterexample, I name Sam Witwicky (*Transformers*, 2007). Sam is—uh—some kid. His dad bought him a car, which happened to be a Transformer. Sam got caught in the plot, but there was no fundamental reason for this particular person to be the protagonist. Even the name is a bit bland for a hero: "Sam Witwicky." Compare that insipid name with the name "Vito Corleone" (The Godfather, 1972). "Vito" means "victorious"; and Corleone means "Lionheart".

So, the hero doesn't have to be The Chosen One, but he can't be just a random guy, either. He has to be "chosen" in the sense that he's the only one who can solve this. He has to be the last hope. If the hero is ordinary, there's no individuation possible because 'ordinary' is the opposite of 'individual.'

*So, how do you make this guy unique?*

Forget genetics and family trees—that's so 20th Century. What a Hero needs is an exceptional talent.

## The Hero's talent

Not all heroes have superpowers. Frodo Baggins's ability was pretty humble: He was more resilient than others to the power of the Ring. Now, supernatural or not, the Hero's talent has these characteristics:

**1) The talent has to be unique.** Only the Villain must share the hero's power—if anyone.

**2) The talent has to be resisted** by the people in the Ordinary World. In the beginning, the hero either hides his powers or uses them to obtain petty advantages.

Examples:

> ***Star Wars:*** Luke sneaks out of the farm to fly his T-16 and meet with his friends. Uncle Lars disapproves.

> ***Harry Potter,*** albeit involuntarily, uses magic at a domestic level, which is forbidden. Uncle Vernon disapproves.
>
> ***The Matrix:*** Neo sells illegal software. If he had an uncle at all, the uncle would surely disapprove.

The Hero's talent follows an arc. At the beginning of the story, not even the Hero understands his own ability: Luke knows nothing about the Force, Neo knows nothing about the Matrix, and Harry knows nothing about magic. But eventually, their skills go from unconscious to conscious. That's because the Hero's talent is part of his personal Shadow, hidden there by the repression of peers, society at large, and/or the Surrogate Parents.

Examples:

> ***Star Wars:*** Uncle Lars and Aunt Beru lied to Luke about his past, denying his origins.
>
> ***Harry Potter:*** Uncle Vernon and Aunt Petunia lied to Harry about his past, denying his origins.
>
> ***The Matrix:*** Neo's boss tells him: *"You believe you are special, that somehow the rules do not apply to you. Obviously, you are mistaken."* But Neo *is* The One. Rules don't apply to him.

## The Hero's power

I lost interest in the movie *Dr. Strange* (2016) at about 30 minutes in. I never finished watching it. The same happened to me with *Green Lantern* (2011). Why? Because in both of them, the Hero had unlimited powers. They could bend time, space, and reality. The consequences of such excesses are unavoidable: Exaggerated twists, plot holes, and implausibility. Whenever you bring multiverses, infinities, and semi-gods into the equation, verisimilitude goes out the window, and the audience goes out the door.

*Heroes* (2006/2010) made the same mistake. *Heroes* was a TV-series about characters so powerful (especially the hero and the villain, who could somehow acquire other mutant's powers) that the story became senseless well before the season's finale.

*Romeo and Juliet* (the original one) isn't about reality bending; it is about tragic love. It was written 400 years ago, and we are still talking about it. I don't think anybody will be talking about *Heroes* or *Dr. Strange* 400 years from now. Heck, I don't think people will be talking about *Green Lantern* 400 seconds from now.

I'd say that the upper limit of power for a hero should be about Superman's level. He is virtually indestructible, but his intelligence is nothing exceptional (as opposed to Lex Luthor's brilliant mind); he is in love with Louise (a weak spot, there); and then there's the kryptonite thing. The more powerful the hero is, the more a "kryptonite factor" is necessary.

If you want a character with unlimited power, it has to be the villain, never the hero, because all-powerful heroes are unrelatable. Leave omnipotence for the gods. Heroes are about human flaws and courage.

## The Hero's day job

Heroes don't just have a regular job. No, sir. Heroes either have a cool job or a terrible one.

The heroes in our examples start their arcs practically as slaves:

> **Star Wars:** Luke has a tough job at the farm and lives under an Imperial dictatorship. Anakin was a slave, too, just like his mother was and like Finn and Rey were (in later episodes of the saga).
>
> **The Matrix:** Neo works for a corporation—not the worst thing in the world. But he is also an oblivious prisoner inside a simulated reality, actually plugged to intravenous hoses in a pod full of slime.
>
> **Harry Potter** is a kid who's bullied, bossed around, and psychologically abused by his surrogate family.

Other heroes (willing heroes, mostly—we will soon see who they are) have interesting jobs; fighter pilots are a classic. However, if the job is cool, then they get fired: Captain Whip Whitaker in *Flight* (2012) got fired; Captain Hal Jordan (*Green Lantern*, 2011) got fired, and Captain Pete Mitchell (*Top Gun*, 2022) got fired. They all are great pilots, and they all got canned.

Another cliché, albeit interesting jobs are: Police officers, FBI or CIA agents, President of the United States, or a woman working as a magazine editor in New York City. (This last one is getting old, though. Why can't a heroine be a brain surgeon or a taxi driver?)

Some heroes have a violent military past. Example: An ex-Black-Ops currently working at a Home Depot (Denzel Washington in *The Equalizer,* 2014), a Navy-Seal working as a cook (Steven Seagal in *Under Siege,* 1992), or Bruce Willis in any of his movies. He's is always an ex-soldier, an ex-cop, or an ex-something who is called upon to save the world.

Now, if the hero's job is both cool and he's doing well in it, then he has some other personal problem. He has to. Example: *Sherlock* (the BBC one) is a consultant detective, which is a super cool job; he's the best, and commissions are not scarce. But he is a pedantic sociopath, bordering on drug-induced psychosis.

Whatever the Hero's job, there has to be a relation between it and the story's mission. For example, if a heroine is a talented wedding planner, the story must involve a wedding, somehow. Say, for instance, that while she's organizing the wedding of some tycoon suspected of financing terrorism, the CIA recruits her to gather intelligence and prevent an upcoming attack. If there's no wedding anywhere, the character's arc will seem disconnected from her backstory.

## The four types of heroes

We saw that villains can adopt non-human forms. Heroes, however, are always human (or at least humanoid, like Pandorians or Kung-Fu Pandas).

Consequently, the following classification of heroes does not relate to their species but to something else: Their attitude regarding the adventure, which in turn is a consequence of how little or much they know about themselves and the world.

Heroes are either **reluctant, tenacious, oblivious,** or **willing**. This classification is important because they all have different origins, motivations, and destinies (see chart on next page).

|  | | |
|---|---|---|
| **High experience** (cool jobs) ➡ | **Reluctant heroes**<br>Defeated, unmotivated | **Tenacious heroes**<br>Focused, motivated |
| **Low experience** (bad jobs) ➡ | **Oblivious heroes**<br>Ignorant, amnesic | **Willing heroes**<br>Motivated but cocky |

Now, with Tom Cruise's help, let's see them in more detail (spoiler alert for the four movies used as examples).

**Reluctant Heroes** stories' are about *duty*. Reluctant Heroes deny or underestimate their abilities, a consequence of their original trauma.

> Example: Lieutenant Daniel Kaffee (Tom Cruise in *A Few Good Men*, 1992) is an unenthusiastic lawyer with a penchant for plea bargains. He rejects to work on a murder in a Military Base; he loses faith, gets drunk, and regrets his decisions, but finally faces the risk of being court-martialed for smearing a high-ranking officer while fulfilling his duty to defending the innocent.

**Oblivious Heroes'** stories are about *identity*. Oblivious Heroes are on a path of discovery, one that starts when they are still a kid or after they lose their memory.

> Example: Commander Jack Harper (Tom Cruise in *Oblivion*, 2013) remembers nothing about the time when he was captured and tricked by an extraterrestrial intelligence into serving its ends. Remembering who he was is the key to

stopping the invasion.

**Tenacious Heroes'** stories are about *willpower.* Tenacious Heroes know something that others don't and must fight despite other people's resistance and disbelief.

> Example: Major William Cage (Tom Cruise in *Edge of Tomorrow,* 2014) is killed in action against the aliens. Then, he awakes back on the morning of that same day, again and again. After having relived that day uncountable times, he knows all that will happen, to the last detail, which is the key to stopping the invasion. He persists and persists until he gets it right.

**Willing Heroes** stories' are about a *mission.* Willing Heroes are overconfident in their abilities. They must learn to put their ego aside and trust a higher power.

> Example: Lt. Pete "Maverick" Mitchell (Tom Cruise in *Top Gun,* 1986) is a pilot competing for the Navy's highest trophy. His cockiness, however, puts him at odds with his colleagues, his trainers, and everyone else. After painful lessons and insights into his own father's past, he achieves a higher reward: Real-life heroism as a pilot, and the acceptance of his brothers in arms.

## The Hero's motive

Heroes always refuse the call to adventure—and then they refuse it again. So why do they finally accept it? Well, it depends on the type of hero. That's how important the classification is.

> **Willing heroes accept the call because it's their job:** Detectives, superheroes, doctors. They can't refuse because protecting the innocent is what they do.
>
> **Reluctant heroes accept the call because they, too, are victims.** Either they are in danger, or someone they love is. Thus, they must defend both themselves and their loved ones, even when they would prefer avoiding confrontation.
>
> **Oblivious heroes accept the call because they need to solve a mystery**, and at the center of that mystery, they will find... Themselves! They, the "Chosen Ones", can't refuse be-

cause it is all a matter self-discovery and fate. (Not unlike psychotherapy, one could say.)

**Tenacious heroes accept the call because of a moral imperative.** They are the protagonists of biopics, true stories, or dramatized historical events. These born leaders can't refuse the call because it is the right thing to do.

No matter their type, heroes are always the underdog, never the establishment. True, some heroes do start at the top of their field (like Stephen Strange in *Doctor Strange*), but in that case, two things happen. First, they fall from heroes to zeros because otherwise there can be no growth. (The fall is the Inciting Event of the story, in the Act I). And second, that field they excel in wasn't their definitive field, after all. Only regular detectives end up being great detectives. Great detectives end up being something else (unless the story has a flat arc).

## Types of heroes arcs

In a fascinating video, writer Kurt Vonnegut explains "The Shapes of Story," which inspired the title of this book.[9] This is the chart he presented as the shape of *Cinderella:*

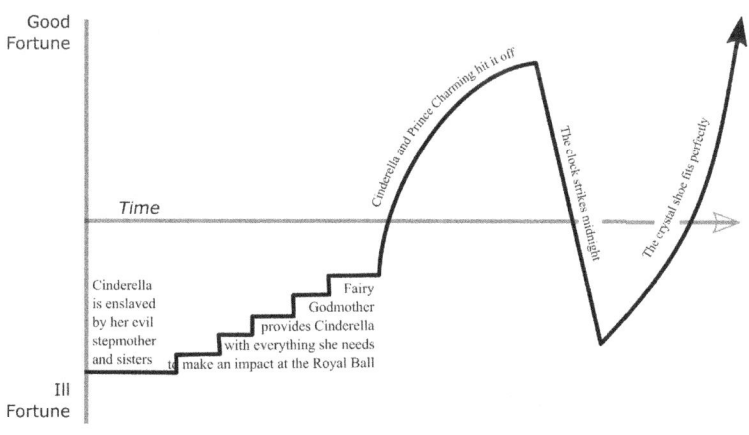

---

9 - https://rebrand.ly/a868c

The graph, however, is incomplete. It barely shows the shape of the Heroine's arc. It doesn't say anything about the villain, the mentor, the Prince Charming, and the rest of the characters. Just as the human psyche is not only about the ego, a story cannot be only about the hero. The shape of *Cinderella*, as a whole, looks a

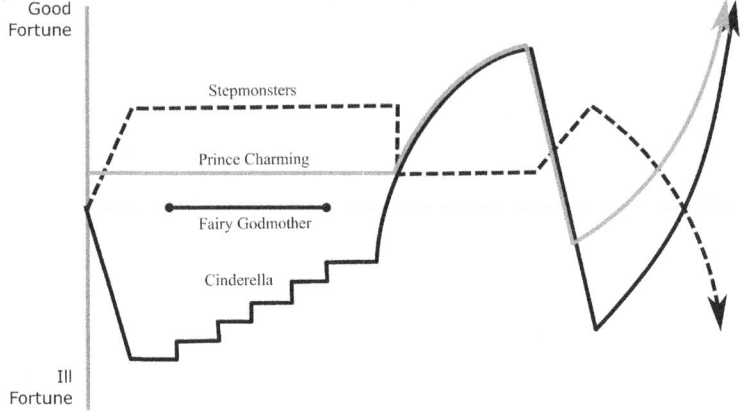

lot more like this:

But let's stay on the Hero's Journey for the moment. For the hero or heroine, There are basically three types of arcs: Positive, flat, and negative.

### **Positive arc**

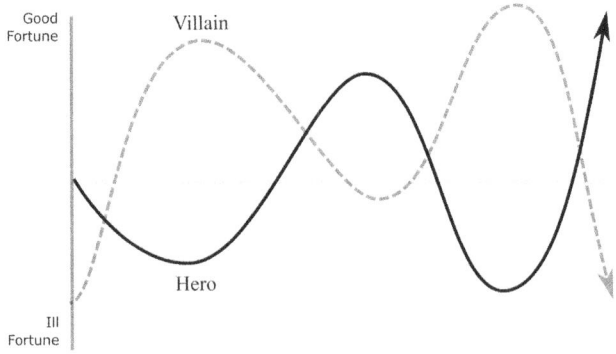

**Stories with a positive arc are about *saving* the world**—or a town, or a family, or whatever that needs saving.

Positive arcs are typical of Willing, Reluctant, and Oblivious heroes. These stories start with the hero as a child (or immature in some other way), and the adventure then transforms this underdog into the person he was born to be. Note how the arcs of the Hero and the Villain flow in symmetrical opposition.

## Flat arc

**Stories with flat arcs are about *changing* the world.**

Flat arcs are typical of Tenacious heroes. They stay true to their convictions even if it spells doom at a personal level. The hero is more knowledgeable and talented than his peers but is nonetheless rejected because of his methods or his personality.

In the end, the Tenacious Hero wins, but there is no glory for him. The reward adopts a more humble shape. Example:

> ***The Hurt Locker*** (2008): Sergeant William James (Jeremy Renner) defuses bombs in Iraq. He is the best, but he is at risk of getting killed by explosions, by enemy soldiers, and eventually even by his comrades, who deem him dangerous and reckless. Things with his wife aren't peachy, either. Eventually, he gets back home to a quiet and peaceful suburban life with his family. But James doesn't feel at home there: He feels at home in the war. In the final scene, we see him walking down a street in Baghdad, headed to disarm yet another bomb, with a satisfied smile on his face.

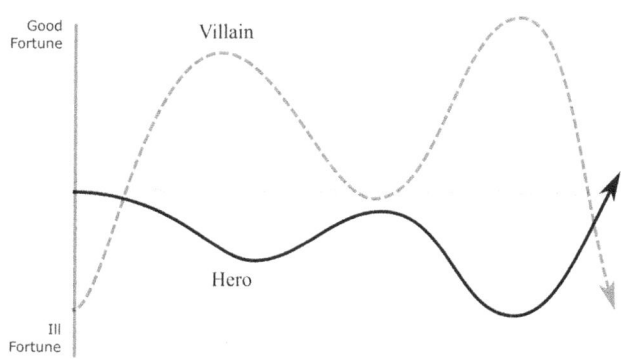

This is how a Hero's "flat" arc looks. Note that it stays on the "ill" part of the chart, except probably at the end.

### Negative arc

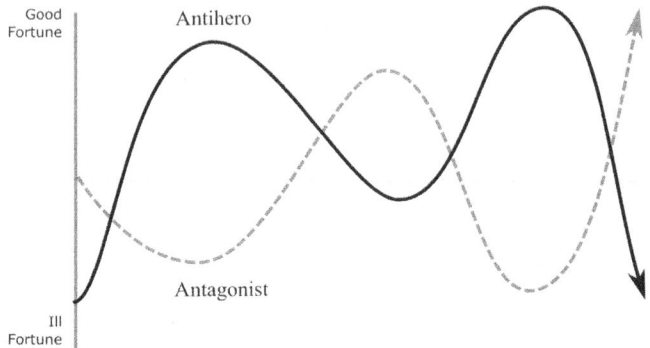

These are the stuff of tragedies, and the protagonist is usually an antihero. A negative arc looks like this:

Note that it looks just the same as the positive arc shown on the previous page, but with the lines of the protagonist and the antagonist interchanged. Example:

> ***In Breaking Bad,*** a terminally-ill chemistry professor starts producing drugs to secure his family's future. Eventually, his health improves, his family grows, and his car wash business flourishes. He could leave the drug business behind, but his moral weakness (his thirst for power) steadily grows inside of him. The more territory he wins in the external world, the more he loses himself. Fatally, it all goes down: His family rejects him, his partners and friends either hate him or get killed, and all that negativity makes his health worsen. His ultimate demise is only cushioned from total disaster by his last-minute, redeeming plan.

What decides the type of arc? What determines if a story ends happily or in tragedy (apart from the author, of course)? The deciding factor is the way the protagonist deals with his *Weakness*.

## The Hero's Weakness

We saw that the cause of the Villain's resentment is repression.

Now, what is the cause of the hero's Weakness?

Simply put, it's **trauma**.

The violent loss of a parent is commonplace. Luke's father was killed (or so he thinks); Hal Jordan's (Green Lantern) father died in a test flight; Dexter's mother was killed; Harry Potter's parents were killed; Bruce Wayne's parents were killed...

The less conscious the trauma is, the most crippling the Weakness is. Consequently, the trauma is not revealed right away but gradually unveiled in the narration, exposing the hero's personality.

As discussed above, the Weakness counterbalances the hero's talent, making him relatable. In any case, the hero's Achilles heel has to be something the audience can identify with. Tip: Antiheroes can even be serial killers and drug traffickers (like Dexter and Walter White), but things like pedophilia and other perversions would never make a character relatable. Avoid completely.

Now, the following chart connects the different types of heroes with their typical weaknesses—a synthesis of the topics discussed in the past sections.

|  | Weakness: | Overcome by: | Apotheosis by: |
|---|---|---|---|
| **Willing** (Ex.: Luke) | Too much self-confidence | Humility and trust in a higher power | Taking a leap of faith |
| **Reluctant** (Ex.: Neo) | Lack of self-confidence | Learn to trust himself | Reaching enlightenment |
| **Oblivious** (Ex.: Harry) | His ignorance about the world | Self-knowledge | Finding identity |
| **Tenacious** (Ex.: Frodo) | Social derision or attack | Resilience | Exercising willpower |

## The Hero's family

In stories about "The Chosen One," we typically have three kinds of parents:

**Biological parents**—the Hero's past. They're almost always dead.

**Surrogate parents,** who belong in the present time and the Ordinary World. These are the proverbial uncle and aunt of so many stories.

**Symbolic parents**, who belong in the journey—in the Adventure World. These characters are usually the Mentor and the Oracle.

The hero becomes the rope of a "tug of war" between opposite worlds: Uncles discourage, mentors encourage; aunts focus on the past; Oracles focus on the future. Mentors and Oracles end up on top, though, because leaving the surrogate home is the first step of becoming a hero by walking one's own path.

## The Hero's Plan-A

The Hero's arc, during the first half of the story, is reactive—he just rolls with the punches. However, he eventually comes up with a plan: Go to the authorities, call the army, compete following the rules, shoot the missiles, or something like that. Plan-A is as reasonable as it is useless.

When does the Hero come up with Plan-A? He does it after his lair (his apartment, his ship, his college dorm, or whatever place he calls home) has been ransacked by the bad guys. That happens at the midpoint of a story (at the precise 50 percent of the way), and it fails at the 62 percent of the way into the story.

*What? At 62 percent? Why not at 63 percent?*

Because of the Golden Ratio (*phi* ≈ 0.618). It relates to the dimensional proportion of the story—the book's length, the movie duration, and so on... But that's a can of worms we will not open for now.

Let's say that if Plan-A were to succeed, the movie would end too soon. Plan-A-must-fail, always.

Examples:

> ***Star Wars:*** "Plan-A" is to rescue Leia from the Death Star. Without titles and credits, the movie is 120 minutes long.
> - At the 60-minute mark (50%), Alderaan (Leia's home) is destroyed.

- At the 74-minute mark (62%), the Imperial troops discover the plan and attack Luke, Leia, Han, and Chewbacca. They fall and get trapped in a trash compactor. R2D2 rescues them; the rescuers have to be rescued.

**The Matrix:** "Plan-A" is to visit the Oracle so she can predict Neo's future. Without titles and credits, the movie is 120 minutes long.
- At the 60-minute mark, Cypher kicks off his plan to attack the Nebuchadnezzar (Neo's new home).
- At the 74-minute mark (62% of 120 minutes), the Agents attack Neo, Morpheus, Trinity, and the rest. They get trapped into the building's walls. Tank rescues them.

**Harry Potter:** "Plan-A" is to play Quidditch (it's a children's movie, after all). Without credits, the movie is 128 minutes long.
- At the 64-minute mark (50% of the way) a Mountain Troll attacks Hogwarts (Harry's new home).
- At the 77-minute mark (62% of 128 minutes), evil Professor Quirrel attacks Harry with dark spells. Harry gets trapped in the middle of the air without control of his broom. Snape rescues him.

*So, what's the point of Plan-A?*

The point is to show the Villain's power and to uncover the crux of his plan. In the meantime, the power of the dark side keeps growing, and the clock is ticking. There's no way back, and this is not working.

We need a Plan-B.

## The Hero's Plan-B

When Plan-A fails, the hero realizes that no one will help. There's no Cavalry; *he* is the Cavalry. And it is clear that the Villain will win. The only good thing, is that now the Hero knows *how* the Villain is going to win.

Plan-B implements the "good death" option, a sacrificial way to stop this, a blow that the Villain will never see coming. It's a long shot, but it has to be tried, even at the cost of one's own life.

That's what heroes do; that's what defines them as such.

In general, Plan-B has these characteristics (I illustrate them using the most relevant dialog from *The Matrix*, Neo's Plan-B):

**Plan-B starts after the Mentor is gone.** Training is over. Now, the Hero must rise to the occasion, he must lead, and he must make his own decisions. (Neo says, *"Stop. I don't believe this is happening."*)

**Plan-B is never fully explained.** It unfolds in real time, creating suspense. (*"The Oracle—she told me this would happen, that I would have to make a choice."*)

**Only the hero believes in the plan;** everyone else thinks he's crazy. (*"Neo, this is* loco. *They've got Morpheus in a military-controlled building."*)

**The plan involves an infiltration,** deep behind enemy lines, sorting all kinds of Gatekeepers. (*"I'm going in"*).

**The plan looks suicidal,** and the Hero is told so. (*"What you're talking about is suicide"*).

Plan-B is brave, but it has a flaw: The Hero wants to protect his friends, so he intends to march alone to the final battle.

That's not going to work. Why?

Because the Hero is brave and powerful, but he cannot pull this off alone. The power of the Villain is too great. He needs his friends, and despite the Hero tries to protect them from the final battle, it is their battle, too. (Trinity says: *"I'm going with you."* Neo says: *"No, you're not."*)

At this point, the "Attack by Ally" happens. Some ally—usually the Goddess—confronts the Hero, and tell him his wrong. This is the final line of this dialog: Trinity tells Neo:

> *"No? Let me tell you what I believe. I believe that Morpheus means more to me than he does to you. I believe if you are really serious about rescuing him, you are going to need my help. And since I am the ranking officer on this ship, if you don't like it, I believe you can go to hell. Because you're not going anywhere else. Tank, load us up."*

That's it, and that's all.

So, Plan-A failed. Plan-B, instead... It fails, too.

*Wait; what? Plan-B fails?!*

Sure it does.

It fails because of the Evil Twist: The Villain always has an ace up his sleeve, so catastrophe ensues.

*But what about stories with a happy end?*

Catastrophe always ensues—even in stories with a happy end. I'll tell you all about it in Chapter 11. For now, let's summarize the Hero's general arc—the Hero's Journey.

## The Hero's general arc - 14 steps

### 1) Humble circumstance, Noble origin.

> **Luke** is a farm boy and the son of the most powerful Jedi.
> **Neo** is a mediocre employee, and the Chosen One.
> **Harry** is a schoolboy, and the Chosen One.

### 2) The Hero is sleeping

> **Luke** is a Willing Hero and a farm boy: he raises early.
> **Neo** is asleep at his computer. "Wake up, Neo."
> **Harry** is asleep. Aunt Petunia: "Up! Get up, now!"

> *Bonus examples:*

> **Ellen Ripley** *(Aliens)* is asleep in a stasis pod.
> **Beatrix Kiddo** *(Kill Bill)* is in a coma.
> **Raleigh Becket** *(Pacific Rim)* is sleeping when the Kaiju alarm sounds.
> (The list of sleeping heroes and heroines is unending.)

### 3) The Hero receives a secret message

> **Luke** discovers a secret holographic message inside R2D2.
> **Neo** receives a secret message on his computer screen.
> **Harry** receives an unexpected flying letter from Hogwarts.

### 4) The Hero meets the Mentor

**Luke** meets Obi-Wan and learns about the Force.
**Neo** meets Morpheus and learns about The Matrix.
**Harry** meets Dumbledore and learns about magic.

## 5) Call to Adventure: Refusal, rebuttal, acceptance.

**Luke** refuses to go to Alderaan—twice.
**Neo** refuses to take the scaffold to the roof.
**Harry** refuses Hagrid's call: "You've made a mistake."

## 6) Road of trials: The Hero fails at first

**Luke** fails the lightsaber training, until he gets it.
**Neo** fails the building jump, but excels in combat.
**Harry** fails in Potions class, but becomes Gryffindor's seeker.

## 7) Plan-A: The Hero and the Goddess barely escape

**Luke and Leia** escape the Death Star.
**Neo and Trinity** escape the Matrix.
**Harry, Ron, and Hermione** escape Fluffy, a three-headed dog.

## 8) Midpoint: Destruction and a key clue

Han Solo's ship is under fire, but they've got the blueprints.
Morpheus Ship is attacked, but Neo has the power of choice.
Hogwarts is under attack, but Harry knows about the Stone.

## 9) Plan-B: The Hero and his team go proactive. They fail.

The Rebels attack the Death Star. They drop like mosquitoes.
The Crew uploads themselves, and it ends up in disaster.
Harry goes for the Stone, and ends up at Quirrell's mercy.

## 10) Plan-C: The Hero knows what to do, but he doesn't say.

**Luke** turns off his targeting computer. *"What's wrong?"* they ask. *"Nothing,"* he says.
**Neo** has a plan. *"What are you doing?"* Trinity asks. He doesn't answer.
**Harry** has a plan. *"You're sneaking out again, aren't you?"* Neville asks. They don't answer.

## 11) Sacrifice: The hero accepts his fate.

Killing the Emperor demands **Luke's death**.
Killing Agent Smith demands **Neo's death**.
Killing Voldemort demands **Harry's death**.

## 12) Resurrection: The Hero can continue fighting.

**Luke** is saved by Han, who shoots Vader's fighter to hell.
**Neo** is saved by Trinity, who confesses her love.
**Harry** comes back thanks to the Resurrection Stone.

## 13) Apotheosis and catharsis: The Hero emerges victorious.

The Death Star explodes in a million pieces.
Smith explodes in a million pieces.
The Dark Lord dissolves into a million pieces.

## 14) Magic flight: The hero flies—for real.

**Luke** flies back to base.
**Neo** flies like Superman.
**Harry** flies on a broom, a hippogriff, or a Ford Anglia. Everything goes. And all the saga's movies end like that.

Yay! Good for the Hero.

And good for the Goddess, too, because without her, he would have never won. Oh, yeah—let's talk about her.

# 5. The Goddess: Don't Mess With The Best

> [SHERLOCK and WATSON are outnumbered and under fire. SHERLOCK just pushed MARY off the moving train.]
>
> WATSON: *Did you kill my wife!? Did you just kill my new wife!?*
>
> SHERLOCK: *Of course not. That was no accident—it was by design. Now, do you need me to elaborate, or can we just crack on?*
>
> (From *Sherlock Holmes: A Game of Shadows,* 2011)

**Heroes fail, fail,** and finally succeed. Goddesses *succeed.*

The Goddess is an angel spoiling for a fight. She is noble, she is intelligent, and she is beautiful (although not necessarily in a stereotypical sense). She is the first of her class; she's the best of them all, which is not to say that she's nice and cute.

Examples:

> ***Star Wars:*** Leia is young, beautiful, brave, and smart. She is a princess, but she resists torture, and she blasts away any Stormtroopers who dare to stand in her way.
>
> ***The Matrix:*** Trinity is young, beautiful, brave, and smart. She will unleash hell on any soldier, policeman, or Agent who dares to stand in her way.
>
> **Harry Potter:** Hermione is young, cute, brave, and smart. She knows all the answers, she excels at all charms, and she will *Petrificus Totalus* the butt of anyone who dares to stand

in her way.

Other goddesses are Leeloo *(The Fifth Element)*, Lois Lane *(Superman)*, Mera *(Aquaman)*, Pepper Potts *(Iron Man)*, Natasha Romanoff *(Avengers)*, Gamora *(Guardians of the Galaxy)*, and a million more. All are young, beautiful, brave, and smart. It's not cliché, it's not stereotypical—it's archetypal.

## The Goddess's wound

We said that Villains come from repression and that Heroes come from trauma. Now, where does the Goddess's resolution come from? What drives her courage?

The Goddess's belligerence and resolution come from loss. She is not fighting for the hero: She is fighting a personal war for justice. It is not resentment—she knows that her actions will not bring her father (or whoever she lost) back. But she fights to heal the world.

She doesn't like to talk about her past, though. She will tell the hero about it, but always in private and only after she learns to trust him.

## The Goddess's Path: From *animus* to *anima*

Note this curious situation: The Goddess represents the feminine, but she still must integrate her own femininity.

At the beginning of many stories, the Goddess adopts an aggressive, "masculine" stance. Why? Simply because at this point the hero isn't around yet, and someone had to rise to the circumstance. She aggressively takes charge of everything, and when the hero shows up, she rejects, demeans, or scolds him.

It is what Jungian psychologists call "a woman in the *animus*," that is, a woman who adopted a masculine role. Jung's disciple and colleague Jolande Jacobi[10] refers to such an "animus-possessed" woman as someone stubborn and argumentative, a female know-it-all who reacts in a masculine way and not intuitively. She criticizes everybody and everything; she's both

---

10 - J. Jacobi - *The Way of Individuation*, p. 115.

annoyed and annoying.

Examples:

> **Star Wars:** Leia bosses Luke and Han around: *"I don't know who you are or where you did come from, but from now on, you do as I tell you, okay?"* Not even Chewbacca, who towers two feet above her, is safe: *"Will somebody get this big walking carpet out of my way?"*

> **The Matrix:** Trinity is in command, second only to the great Morpheus. Her annoyance is most patent when she interacts with Cypher, but in general, she doesn't talk much—she first shoots, and then asks questions (if there's someone left to answer them).

> **Harry Potter:** Hermione's bosses Ron and Harry around: *"You two better change into your robes. I expect we'll be arriving soon,"* or *"You've got dirt on your nose, did you know?"* Annoyance is *h*er default mood, and the proof is a YouTube video titled *Hermione Being Annoyed for 8 Movies Straight.*[11]

The key for a woman to return to her femininity, according to Dr. Jacobi (a woman herself), lies in using that momentary masculine, cold objectivity to take a hard look at her own Shadow so that she can see the difference between herself and her opinions, between her feminine self and her masculine animus.

When can the Goddess return to her feminine attitude? Only when the (initially) immature Hero eventually steps up to his masculine role. The Hero must divert his attention from her (the fascination that the Goddess presence causes in him) and focus on the task at hand. There is always a step in the individuation of a woman (now is Dr. Jung speaking) in which, if she wants to acquire an individual personality, she must give up the magic power she possesses over men on account of their projection of their own anima on her.

The arc of the Goddess (or the Prince Charming—the masculine version of the soul-image archetypes) involves her getting trapped, held captive, locked in, locked out, stuck, or in some other way blocked from fighting in the final battle because that's a

---

*11 - https://rebrand.ly/x42ju5x*

task reserved for the Hero (or the Heroine). This resonates with traditional tales, in which the anima character saves herself by escaping from a negative masculine figure (an ogre, an evil wizard, and so on). According to Louise Marie Von Franz, escaping from her masculine side is the way a woman reunites with her femininity. In short, she has to stop acting like a man, and she has to stop being a woman by mere opposition to men. Also, the return of the Goddess to femininity (and her acceptance of the Hero) happens right after they fight and win together. Don't think that this return to femininity remotely implies any loss of power; on the contrary, she becomes more focused and fearless. She's now fully in the role of the anima.

Examples:

> **Star Wars:** Only when they are fighting together to evade the Stormtroopers chasing them, Leia gently kisses Luke's cheek, wishing him luck, before a *jump* over an abyss. She also hugs Chewbacca after they repel the imperial fighters and *jump* to hyperspace. This is when she "jumps" from captive princess to true leader of the Resistance.
>
> **The Matrix:** After fighting side by side on skyscrapers rooftops, Trinity goes from crew-mate to acting captain, and from running away from the Agents to shooting them in the freaking head. She's not running away anymore; she can take her place next to Neo to form an invincible team.
>
> **Harry Potter:** It took eight movies and an excruciating battle together for Hermione to kiss Ron. She just went from nerdy know-it-all, to destroyer of horcruxes and certified Death-Eaters' butt-kicker.

Remember: the goddess is not the Hero's anima; she steps up from "being in the animus" to being the story's anima. Hero and Goddess become the heart and the soul of the story (*anima* is Latin for 'soul').

## Non-human feminine figures

Surprise quiz! Who was the Goddess in *Star Trek - The Original Series*?

(Hint: It wasn't a person.)

Captain Kirk wasn't attached to any woman in particular; instead, he was sort of an interplanetary Casanova. Spock had no romantic interests, and he ignored Nurse Chapel's innuendos. Chapel and Uhura were the only stable female characters in the series, but (not surprisingly for the times) their roles were minor. They, ergo, weren't true Goddesses.

*So, there was no Goddess in Star Trek?*

Yes, there was. The goddess was the Enterprise. The ship's influence on Kirk's personality was noticeable: As long as he was sitting at the bridge, he was bold, balanced, and confident; the moment he was off-board, things changed.[12]

Star Trek - The New Generation, on the contrary, had two human Goddesses: Deanna Troi and Beverly Crusher. But come to it, Picard also had this anima-like connection to the ship, symbolized by his strict sense of duty. Also, this version of the Enterprise now had a female voice, too (Majel Barrett's voice, actress and wife of Gene Roddenberry, the creator of the series—his Goddess, we could say).

By the way—note the choice of names for Picard goddesses: *Treu,* in German (pronounced "troi"), means loyal, faithful. And the Captain and Dr. Crusher had a "crush" on each other.

## The Goddess's main functions

There are two things the Goddess does that no one else can:

1) She resurrects the hero.

2) She guides the Hero back home after the final battle.

The Goddess anchors the hero (the ego) to reality, preventing him from ego inflation.

*Sounds great. Why isn't the Goddess the main character, then?*

Because being The Goddess is not a question of gender but a matter of functions. She helps and counterbalances the Hero, just like the soul-image archetype compensates and helps us in our dreams.

---

*12 - Kenneth L. Golden - Science Fiction, Myth, and Jungian Psychology - Edwin Mellen Press, 1995.*

The character of the Goddess can provide the POV (point of view) for the story, though. For example, *The Quick and the Dead* (1995) tells the story from the Goddess's perspective ("The Lady," portrayed by Sharon Stone), but the Hero is Cort (portrayed by Russell Crowe).

Now, there are a million stories with a female lead, but if she genuinely is the protagonist, then she's not a Goddess but a Heroine.

## Goddesses vs. Heroines

Examples of heroines are Katniss Everdeen *(The Hunger Games)*, Ellen Ripley *(Aliens)*, Furiosa *(Mad Max, 2015)*, and Beatrix Kiddo *(Kill Bill)*. Also, Lara Croft, Elizabeth Bennet, Bridget Jones, Wonder Woman, and every female superhero and Disney Princess out there.

These are the differences between Goddesses and Heroines:

**1) Goddesses first enter the scene as a magical apparition,** evident in her attire and in some magical manifestation that causes awe in the Hero. Examples:

> ***Star Wars:*** Leia shows up as a ghostly, magic-like apparition—the blue hologram. Luke is amazed: *"Who's she? She's beautiful!"*
>
> ***Harry Potter:*** Hermione shows up in her Hogwarts robe, haughty and dignified, literally performing magic *("Oculus reparo!")*. Harry and Ron are amazed.
>
> ***The Matrix:*** Trinity dresses in an awesome leather outfit and jumps from wall to wall and between buildings. *"That's impossible,"* says a police officer in awe. Later she stuns Neo, when he discovers that she is *"the Trinity, the one* (The One?) *who cracked the IRS database"*.

Heroines, instead, enter the scene as ordinary people because the Hero's Journey starts in the Ordinary World. For example, Rey *(Star Wars)* scavenges parts from derelict ships; Tess McGill *(Working Girl,* 1988) travels on a jam-packed ferry on her way to work as an assistant; and so on. Many heroines start their stories literally sleeping, or getting out of bed, as many male heroes do.

**2) Goddesses rarely have a family** (except for the proximity to the Mentor, her Surrogate Father of sorts).

**3) Heroines have companions, Goddesses don't:** A sidekick, a comic-relief character, an android, a best friend, or an animal.

**4) Goddesses are naturally distrusting;** the wounds of the past made them so. Heroines, instead, can be overly trusting (Snow White, The Little Mermaid, Sleeping Beauty, and so on) until they learn better.

**5) Goddesses can revert the effects of the dark side,** which shows in the scene in which they resuscitates the Hero. Heroines, instead, are vulnerable to evil.

**6) Goddesses cannot defeat the Villain.** Only Heroines can.

The worst that can happen to a leading female character is being neither a Goddess nor a Heroine. I think this is the problem in every *Charlie's Angels* movie ever made: The characters were shallow, grown women with an adolescent attitude, not fitting any of the two archetypes.

*Do Heroines have a Goddess on their team?*

No, they don't. They have, instead, a Prince Charming—or two.

## The Prince Charming

The Heroine is already in charge of the feminine energy in the story, so the soul-image character has to be a male (a good *animus*) embodying the masculine energy.

The positive animus is stereotypically represented as an idealized man: Handsome, supporting, objective, rational, calm, and confident. This character (like the anima) comes from nobility: He is a prince, or a millionaire, or a millionaire's heir. Introduce him to your mom, and she will tell you that he's the ideal candidate for you. That's why I call this character "Prince Charming." (Well, because of that, and because of Disney's stereotype, too.)

The animus can have a negative version, though, like all archetypes, in which case they gain interest. My favorite animus ever was mind-reading, psychopath, anthropophagous Dr. Hannibal Lecter, who helped FBI trainee heroine Clarice Starling catch a serial killer in *The Silence of the Lambs* (1991).

Yeah, no, please don't introduce Hannibal Lecter to your mom—trust me on this one.

The following are examples of *animi*. As pointed out by Von Franz, in traditional tales, the role of the animus is sometimes represented not by one but by two (and sometimes more) male characters. The same happens in movies:

> **Star Wars - Episode VII** (2015): Rey is the heroine, and the good animuses are Finn and Dameron Poe.
>
> **Rogue One** (2016): Jyn Erso is the heroine, and the good animuses are Cassian Andor and the rest of the ship's crew (all men), which double in other functions, as well.
>
> **Wonder Woman** (2018): Diana is the heroine, and the good animus is young, handsome, calm, clever, handsome spy Steve Trevor.
>
> **The Terminator** (1984): The good *animus* is courageous time-traveler Kyle Reese. Interesting fact: in this movie, Sarah Connor was the heroine, but in *Terminator 2* (1991), she was the Goddess.
>
> **The Hunger Games** (2012): The good *animuses* are Peeta and Gale. Young, clever, calm. And handsome.

Yes, they're all handsome. Also, just like the Goddess restores life to the Hero, the animus-character often "resurrects" the Heroine with a waking-up kiss, a crystal shoe, or some other intervention. Such commonplaces have 'Disney' written all over them.

## Male "Goddesses"

*What? Male Goddesses?*

Yes. There is a difference between a Prince Charming (a man functioning as an animus) and a Male "Goddess" (a man functioning as an anima).

For example, in *Indiana Jones and the Last Crusade* (1989), there is no Goddess character; the only woman here is a "Witch"—Nazi archaeologist Elsa Schneider. However, the role of the Goddess has to be fulfilled by someone.

Enter Marcus Brody and Dr. Henry Jones (played by Denholm Elliot and Sean Connery). Despite these characters being male, they are mild-mannered gentlemen; they are trapped (typical of Goddesses) inside a huge tank, and during the fight that ensues, the Nazi soldiers laugh at them: *"These Americans, they fight like women!"*

They, however, take control of the tank, save Indiana Jones's life, and enable him to keep fighting—just like a regular Goddess would. Note that despite being men, they aren't animuses but animas because they complement not a woman but a male Hero.

The Nazi soldiers? They are permanently unavailable for comment on the matter. Goddesses get things done—even if they happen to be seventy-odd years old men. Their underestimation was typical of dark side minor characters toward women (*"We can take care of one little girl"* says a police lieutenant, and Trinity proceeds to kill them all).

## The Goddess's arc, step-by-step

These steps are presented chronologically here; however, the order of these stages in a story can change because of non-linear narratives. Also, note that this arc is relevant to Goddesses only; Heroines follow the Hero's arc (page 55).

1. **Special origin. The Goddess was born to a royal (or foreign, or noble, or somehow special) family, and her name has religious connotations.**

   **Leia** is the Princess of Alderaan and Queen Amidala's daughter. Her name means "child of heaven."
   **Trinity** carries a divine association in her name (the Holy Trinity).
   **Hermione** was born to a Muggle family, but her name is the feminine of Hermes, the Greek messenger god.

2. **The Goddess's loss: She either lost someone violently, or**

**she has no family anymore.**

**Leia** lost all their parents—biological, surrogate, and symbolic.
**Trinity** has no family, and now Morpheus was taken away from her.
**Hermione,** resigned to die, performs the *Obliviate* spell on her parents, effectively "losing" them that way.

## 3. The Goddess is "in the animus," embarked on a war of her own. She doesn't care much yet about the Hero.

**Leia** is fighting a war. She doesn't care who Luke and Han are.
**Trinity** was fighting even before Neo entered the scene.
**Hermione** is fighting not for Harry, but for Hogwarts.

## 4. The Goddess is trapped by a male figure.

**Leia** is captured and held prisoner in the Death Star.
**Trinity**'s call was traced; she's trapped in The Matrix.
**Hermione** is trapped in the bathroom with a Mountain Troll.

## 5. The Goddess resists the power of the dark animus. She is on the floor, literally, and she cannot fight. But she resists.

**Leia** lies down in a cell. Vader tortures her. She resists.
**Trinity** falls to the floor, down some stairs. *"Get up, Trinity. Get. Up."*
**Hermione** resists the troll's attack hiding on the floor under a lavatory.

## 6. The Goddess tests the Hero. He fails.

**Leia** asks Luke, *"Aren't you a little short for a Stormtrooper?"* Luke just stands there, dumbfounded.
**Trinity** scans Neo for tracking devices. He was indeed "bugged."
**Hermione** tests Ron. *"Oh, are you doing magic? Let's see then."* His spell doesn't work.

## 7. The Goddess escapes with the help of the Hero and the Sidekick.

**Leia** is rescued by Luke and Han.
**Trinity** is rescued from the helicopter crash by Neo (and Tank).
**Hermione** is saved by Harry and Ron, who defeat the troll.

8. **The Goddess accepts the Hero after fighting and winning together.**

> **Leia, Luke,** and **Han** repel an enemy attack. They are a team now.
> **Trinity, Neo,** and **Morpheus** converge on a skyscraper's rooftop. They are a team now.
> **Harry, Ron,** and **Hermione** defeat the Troll. They are a team now. Five points for Gryffindor!

9. **The Goddess has a secret. I can't tell you about it, but it is about love. Okay, I'm going tell you: She's in love.**

> **Leia** is in love. She doesn't tell, because Han is materialistic, sarcastic, and arrogant.
> **Trinity** is in love. She doesn't tell, because it was a prediction made by the Oracle for her ears only.
> **Hermione** is in love. She doesn't tell, because Ron is dating Lavender Brown.

10. **The Goddess saves the hero.**

> **Leia** resuscitates Han Solo from the carbonite.
> **Trinity** resuscitates Neo, allowing him to keep fighting.
> **Hermione** resuscitates Ron, wounded while escaping the Ministry of Magic.

11. **The Goddess restitutes the Hero his heart, either figuratively (he gives him hope, or love) or she gives him a literal, freaking heart.**

> In *Iron Man* (2008), Obadiah Stane takes Tony's nuclear-powered heart from his chest, leaving him for dead. **Pepper Pots** gives Tony the heart he made back in the cave in Afghanistan.
> In *Notting Hill* (1999), William got his heart broken. Anna visits him at the bookstore and presents him with a painting about love, as a way to say that she's sorry, and offering her heart to him. This inspires him to march to the final battle. (See the painting on page 71).
> In *The Matrix,* Agent Smith shoots Neo in the heart. Trinity confesses her love for him, and his heart starts beating again, allowing him to march into the final battle.

12. **The Goddess declares her love.**

> **Leia** says it: *"I love you."*
> **Trinity** says it: *"I love you."*

In *Harry Potter,* there are no literal "I love you's," but both Ron and Harry get kisses with a clear message attached to them.

## 13. The Goddess finds herself locked or stuck—again. She can't join the final battle, but the Hero delivers.

**Leia** is stuck on planet Yavin, about to be destroyed. Luke blows up the Death Star and saves her (and everyone else, too.)
**Trinity** is stuck in the ship, about to be killed by a Sentinel. Neo destroys Smith and saves her (and everyone else, too.)
**Hermione** is locked out from the final battle. Harry destroys Voldemort and saves her (and everyone else, too.)

## 14. The Goddess guides the hero back to the real world.

**Leia** orders the fleet (including Luke's ship) back to the base.
**Trinity** screams at Neo to take the phone call. He awakes in the real world, in her arms.
**Hermione,** off-screen, brings back Ron and Harry (who were left unconscious after the battle for the Sorcerer's Stone).

## 15. The Goddess and the hero achieve union.

**Leia** learns that she and Luke are brother and sister, and she renews her love with Han.
**Trinity**'s union with Neo is symbolized simply by a kiss. Classic.
**Hermione** marries Ron, and Harry marries Ginny Weasley (a minor-Goddess character).

## 16. The Goddess finds a new family.

**Leia** was alone; now she has found a new family.
**Trinity** has was alone; now she found love in Neo.
**Hermione** has found love in Ron and a family in the Weasleys.

A word about the union of the Goddess and the Hero: This is about love, but not necessarily about romantic love, like in the typical "and they lived happily ever after" ending—Cinderella style. (By the way, Cinderella is not a goddess but a heroine.)

For example, in *Interstellar* (2014), Cooper, for whom only a couple of years have passed, reunites with his daughter Murph, already an older woman on her deathbed, in an emotive embrace that represents the integration of the soul-image to consciousness, an essential step in the individuation process.

Also, as detailed in the last step in the Goddess's arc, the Goddess and Hero don't rise to the Higher Realm like the Mentor and the Oracle do. The Goddess and the Hero aren't mana personalities; they are and stay human.

Last example: *In The Lord of the Rings: The Return of the King* (2003), Frodo ascends to the High Realm, but the other two heroes remain in the real world, united to their respective goddesses: Aragorn with Lady Arwen at his side and Samwise Gamgee with Rosie Cotton at his.

*(I'm not crying. I just got something in the eye.)*

Marc Chagall, *La Mariée* (The Bride) - 68 × 53 cm, 1950. (Fair use.) Note the archetypical and symbolic richness of the painting.

# 6. The Mentor: Venerable But Deceiving

> *"The problem with Internet quotes is that you can't always depend on their accuracy."*
>
> -Sir Isaac Newton, 1684

If there were a job description for being a Mentor, it would look like this:

1) Send a herald to find you a hero. 2) Convince the hero to march to the adventure. 3) Train the hero, and point him toward the bad guy. 4) Until the hero's ready, protect them with your life.

There is another task, though: Convincing everyone else to go ahead with this plan, which is both high-cost and high-risk. So, the Mentor is himself a Tenacious Hero of sorts because he must overcome the resistance of the members of the Higher Realm.

Examples:

> ***Star Wars*:** In The Empire Strikes Back (1980), Obi-Wan has to convince Yoda (a member of the Higher Realm) to train Luke despite the old master's objections. *"I cannot teach him. The boy has no patience."* Mace Windu rejected Anakin's training. *"He's too old."*
>
> ***The Matrix:*** In *The Matrix Reloaded* (2003), Morpheus has to convince the High Council to let him take Neo to see the Oracle despite the impending invasion.

***Harry Potter***: Dumbledore dissipates McGonagall's objections about Hagrid (*"I would trust Hagrid with my life,"* he says) and about leaving Harry with the Dursleys. Also, he has to act despite the opposition of the Ministry of Magic.

## The Mentor's Call to Adventure

The Call to Adventure is an essential part of the first act of any story. It always results in a back-and-forth of refusals and rebuttals between the Hero and the Mentor. The Hero finally accepts the call when he understand that he (or people he loves) are already at risk because of the dark side actions.

The whole discussion not always take long, especially if the story is about a Willing Heroes or a Tenacious Heroes. In the movie *Inside Man* (2006), the whole Call to Adventure takes seventeen seconds. Detective Frasier (Denzel Washington) sits at his desk when the captain arrives. His partner, Detective Mitchell, is also there.

> CAPTAIN: *Christmas came early for you. Bank robbery. Hostages.*
>
> FRASIER: *What?* [First refusal.]
>
> CAPTAIN: *Grossman's on vacation. You're up.*
>
> FRASIER: *What about the Madrugada cheque-cashing thing? I thought I was in the doghouse.* [Second refusal.]
>
> CAPTAIN: *I just threw you a bone. As far as I'm concerned, you still work here, but if you don't think you're ready--*
>
> MITCHELL: *No, no, he's ready!* [Mitchell answers the call for Frasier before he has the chance to reject it again.]

The Captain here functions as both the Herald (he "finds" the hero) and the "Mentor" in that he makes the Call and manages the refusals. Detective Frasier is a Tenacious Hero: going into the adventure is his job, after all. Consequently, the call is short, and the Mentor is a minor character. On the other extreme, the Call to Adventure in Star Wars takes 24 minutes, between the moment Luke first meets the Heralds (the two droids) up to the moment he tells Obi-Wan that he will go to planet Alderaan and learn the ways of the Force.

## The Mentor's wisdom

We said Mentors are wise—an embodiment of the Wise Old Man archetype. So, how does the wisdom of the mentor manifest? Like this.

**The Mentor is a good listener,** but he doesn't force confessions. Dumbledore tells Harry: *"Is there anything you'd like to tell me—anything at all?"* Harry: *"No, professor. Nothing."* Dumbledore once asked Tom Riddle the same question. *"No, sir, nothing,"* Tom answered. Dumbledore looked them in the eye but didn't insist.

**The Mentor never reacts with anger.** He can indeed overreact (especially in comedies, like Doc Brown in Back to the Future), but never angrily.

**The Mentor never panics.** He shows concern and even fear; he's human, after all, but he never loses control of himself.

**The Mentor follows his conviction blindly.** In *The Matrix,* the Oracle tells Neo that Morpheus believes in him "so blindly, that no one can convince him otherwise, not even me."

## The Mentor's deceit

The problem with the Mentor's words is that you can't depend on their accuracy. He's not just a benevolent, nice older man: There's an element of deceit in him.

Look at the Jedi Order from Star Wars. They recruit kids as young as three years old, separating them from their families for good and sending them away to a compound full of adult men who spend all day waggling lightsabers. And once you're in the Jedi program, you don't get to opt out, ever. Obi-Wan tells 19-year-old Anakin, "You made a commitment to the Jedi Order, a commitment not easily broken." No, Obi-wan, he didn't: When you recruited him as an indentured servant, he was just a kid.

So you see, The Jedi Order, "the guardians of peace and justice in the galaxy," is actually an irrevocable cult that lands somewhere between a forced boot camp and human trafficking.36

Also, the Mentor knows that the Hero will die in order to win this. So their job description should also include the task of "priming the Hero for sacrifice." Or at least, he should say something about it. Jung warns us about the powerful fascination the two mana archetypes emanate:

> They lure one into a kind of self-glorification and megalomania until one is able, by making them conscious and distinguishing oneself from them, to break free from the danger of identification with their delusive image.[13]

The Mentor's deceitful ways are a good example of this archetype's dual nature, dual as a Yin and Yang symbol—half white, half black, but inside the white area, there's a fat, dark spot.

## The Mentor's arc, step-by-step

This is what happens with Mentors in all stories. As always, this are symbolic milestones; the particular way in which a story implements the steps will be dictated by its genre and by the author's imagination.

1. **Historical war: the mentor is a veteran of an old war.**

    **Obi-Wan** is a veteran of the Clone Wars.
    **Morpheus** is a veteran and a leader in the Resistance.
    **Dumbledore** is a veteran of the First Wizarding War.

2. **The mentor awaits nearby for the right moment.**

    **Obi-Wan** has been living all these years very close to Luke.
    **Morpheus** says he spent his entire life looking for Neo.
    **Dumbledore** keeps Harry in hiding in Little Whinging.

3. **The Mentor first meets the Hero in a protected place.**

    **Luke** meets Obi-Wan in a cave in the desert.
    **Morpheus** meets Neo in an abandoned hotel.
    **Dumbledore** welcomes Harry at Hogwarts.

4. **The Mentor scares away enemies, or commands respect.**

    **Obi-Wan** shows up and the Sand People run away in fear.
    **Morpheus**'s presence commands the crew's respect.
    **Hagrid** (acting as Herald and first "Mentor") shows up and

---

13 - J. Jacobi – *The Psychology of C.G. Jung* - p.126

scares away the dark figures in Knockturn Alley.

### 5. The Mentor talks about the backstory and the Prophecy.

**Obi-Wan** tells Luke about how Vader betrayed the Jedi Order.
**Morpheus** tells Neo about the prophecy of The One.
**Hagrid** tells Harry about his parents and about the prophecy.

### 6. The Mentor doesn't say everything he knows.

**Obi-Wan** tells Luke half-truths about his father.
**Morpheus** doesn't tell Neo what The Matrix is. *"You have to see it for yourself,"* he says.
**Dumbledore,** who knows everything, and says very little.

### 7. The Proper Call to Adventure.

**Obi-Wan** asks Luke to go to Alderaan with him.
**Morpheus** shows Neo the red and the blue pills.
**Hagrid** tells Harry to follow him.

### 8. The Mentor trains the hero. They are already in the Adventure World, at the Hero's new home.

**Obi-Wan** trains Luke aboard the Millennium Falcon.
**Morpheus** trains Neo aboard the Nebuchadnezzar.
**Harry** receives training at Hogwarts.

### 9. Baptism of fire. The Mentor issues an order that must absolutely be followed.

**Obi-Wan** tells Luke, *"Your destiny lies along a different path than mine. The Force will be with you always."*
**Morpheus** tells Trinity, *"Get Neo out. He's all that matters."*
**Dumbledore** orders Harry to hide under the floor of the Astronomy Tower, no matter what happens.

### 10. The Mentor attracts the fight to him so the Hero can escape.

Obi-Wan attracts the fight to him. "Run, Luke, Run!"
Morpheus attracts the fight to him. "Trinity, go!"
Dumbledore attracts the fight to him (Draco's *expelliarmus* and Snape's *Avada Kedavra*). "Severus, I beg you."

### 11. The Mentor is gone. He leaves a crucial legacy for the Hero.

**Obi-Wan** is stricken down.

**Morpheus** is beaten and taken prisoner.
**Dumbledore** falls.

12. **The Mentor's words resound in the Hero's mind, and those words are about *choice.***

    **Obi-Wan:** *"Use the Force, Luke!"* Luke chooses to use the force instead of his starfighter's targeting computer.
    **Morpheus:** *"When you are ready, you won't have to* [dodge bullets]*"* The Matrix is all about the The One's choice; that's the core of its premise.
    **Dumbledore:** *"It is our choices, Harry, that show what we truly are, far more than our abilities."*

13. **The Mentor ascends to the Higher Realm; after his sacrifice, the Mentor reaches a (literal or figurative) supernatural state. An aura of white or blue light surrounds him.**

    **Obi-Wan** shows up as a ghost, surrounded by the blue light of the Force.
    **Morpheus** returns from the Matrix to the Real World via a Public Telephone. He dissolves in an aura of blue light.
    **Dumbledore** returns as an apparition, surrounded by white light.
    Bonus example:
    **Gandalf** returns as Gandalf The White, surrounded by light.

And that covers the arc of the Mentor. The challenge is to create a story that intertwines all the arcs presented (the Hero's, the Goddess's, the Mentor's), with the plan of the Villain, and with the rest of the characters.

Hey—nobody said that it was going to be easy. If you want easy, you'd better go collecting stamps or something.

Writing is for the brave.

# 7. Designing The Rest Of The Characters

*"Some people play hard to get. I play hard to want."*

(From *The Adventures of Ford Fairlane,* 1990.)

**Not all antagonists are evil.** In some stories, they can be sports rivals, natural enemies, hungry animals, a certain life situation, or a certain character's weakness. But even when they are intelligent and truly villainous beings, they are given a chance to make things right.

Grand Villains are different. You never offer a Grand-villain the chance to reconsider. That would be like an insult to him, because he's the devil.

Grand-villains aren't evil because of some narcissistic *boo-boo.* There are no reasons, no regrets, and not much backstory, either. They represent the negative pole in the theme—a primordial absolute. They are evil just because.

Note that a Grand-villain and a supervillain are two different things: A supervillain is just a villain with superpowers, and a Grand-villain is the Villain's mentor, boss, or master.

Examples of Grand-villains are:

> **The Joker** (*The Dark Night,* 2008) doesn't care about money or power. And boy—he's a psycho. There's no explanation for his actions or his scars; he just makes up a different story each time. As Alfred says, *"Some men only want to see the world burn."*

**Voldemort** isn't fighting for anything or anyone. He is not trying to achieve any ultimate "good"—or whatever perverted idea of good that he might have. He is an example of a Villain and a Grand-villain fused in one character.

**The Dark Planet** (a.k.a. The Great Evil), from *The Fifth Element* (1997), brings destruction without explanation: It is the ultimate, non-human form of Grand-villain. Thank God for Zorg (Gary Oldman), who brought to the movie all the intelligence, arrogance, and touch of humor that an unforgettable villain needs.

## The Sidekick

When they said, "An old friend will help you move; a best friend will help you move a dead body," they were talking about the Sidekick. He is an ally one-hundred-percent loyal to the Hero.

My favorite sidekick is Samwise Gamgee from *The Lord of the Rings*. As they approach Mount Doom, the Ring takes a rising toll on Frodo to the point that he cannot walk anymore. *"Come, Mr. Frodo!"* Sam cries. *"I can't carry it for you, but I can carry you!"*

In our example stories, the sidekicks are:

*Star Wars:* R2D2, who will cross a desert to fulfill his mission, and will ride Luke's starfighter to help him in the battle.

*The Matrix:* Tank, who follows orders without questions and saves his friends at the cost of his own life.

*Harry Potter* has two Sidekicks; one is Ron Weasley, who frequently questions Harry, which is atypical of a Sidekick. So we also have Hedwig, a loyal messenger owl who always helps Harry and ultimately gives its life to protect him.

Remember the "Attack by Ally" stage (page 54)? The Hero is told that his obsession is taking him nowhere and that he cannot fight this alone. Well, such recrimination is never made by the Sidekick because sidekicks are unconditional. In fact, in some stories, the Sidekick is not human, which explains the lack of moral independence of this character. Examples of non-human sidekicks (other than androids and owls) are:

In ***Iron Man*** (2008), Tony Stark's sidekick is Jarvis, an artificial intelligence.

In ***Dredd*** (2012), Judge Dredd (Karl Urban) is the mentor, and Judge Anderson (Olivia Thirlby) is the heroine. The sidekicks are their intelligent weapons.

Cars can be sidekicks—like Herbie, in **Herbie the Love Bug,** or K.I.T.T. in the ***Knight Rider*** TV series.

## The Lieutenants

The term 'Lieutenants' is symbolic; they don't have to be in the military, of course. I call them "lieutenants" because they have the power in *lieu* of the Villain. And they don't have to be human, either; the small asteroids impacting Earth before the killer asteroid arrives in *Armageddon* (1998) are "lieutenants," too.

Many authors make the mistake of designing clumsy Lieutenants, like those generic Henchmen that fall to the floor like a sack of potatoes after just one karate chop.

Well-designed Lieutenants, instead, are strong and terrifying, forcing the hero to fight hard past them to reach the final boss of the game.

Examples of both types of lieutenants:

> ***Star Wars:*** Stormtroopers are pretty dorky, really. Imperial pilots were a bit better, but still not very frightening. My favorite lieutenant in the saga was Darth Maul—while he lasted.
>
> In ***The Matrix,*** the Agents are indestructible and relentless. Scary.
>
> In ***Harry Potter,*** we have Death Eaters, Dementors, and the evilest witch in the world. We also have giant spiders, serpents, and even werewolves. Fantastic.

In general, a lieutenant is whatever/whoever carries out the dirty work of the villain, but the chief lieutenant is a character I call "the Witch."

Talk about scary!

## The Witch

She is the evil version of the Goddess. In the same way that the Goddess is the most proficient among the good guys, the Witch is the most devious among the bad guys.

In modern stories, Witches don't look "Halloweeny" at all, like those old women with an owl on their shoulders and a pointy hat. Witches these days can be businesswomen, lawyers, mutants, ninjas, or pageant queens.

The Harry Potter series has many witches because the story happens to be about magic, but the story, in narrative terms, has one Witch (uppercase 'W'): Bellatrix Lestrange.

In The Matrix and Star Wars, the Witch character is not present, although I remember seeing some early conceptual sketches for a Sith witch, made for Lucas Films. The sketches were so terrifying that the figure got excluded from the movies, which were intended to appeal to children, too.

Batman stories feature Witches in a rather histrionic way. In those movies, there is always a male Villain (The Joker, The Penguin, Mr. Freeze, and so on) who have a Witch as an accomplice, girlfriend, or lieutenant (Harley Quinn, Catwoman, Poison Ivy, and so on). Everyone's got a costume.

*What does the Witch want? Power? Revenge?*

No. What the Witch wants is **sadistic pleasure.** People have to die and suffer because of the pleasure she experiences by inflicting pain. These are some other typical aspects of this character:

**The Witch has no backstory,** which would give her a reason to be evil—a human dimension of sorts. She has none.

**The Witch doesn't talk much** unless it is to hurt with her words.

**The Witch is rarely a False Enemy or a Traitor** because those characters work surreptitiously. Not the Witch: she's way too devoted to the dark side to pretend otherwise.

**The Witch is *not* the Villain;** there are certainly female Villains, who follow the Villain's archetype described in Chapter 3. But the Witch, as a character, lacks the necessary depth for that.

She's here to inflict fear and pain, only—and to die in a cathartic way that makes the audience happy. As a matter of karma, since the Witch causes suffering, she has to die a horrible death. (Remember, it doesn't have to be a literal death, but it has to be something terrible.)

*Who kills the Witch?*

The hero or heroine does, and more rarely, the Goddess does. (Exception: *Mission Impossible - Ghost Protocol,* 2011, in which Agent Carter kicks Sabine Moreau out of a window on the 100th floor of a skyscraper.

*Is there a male version of the Witch?*

Yes. A female Villain many times has a male "witch" at her side. I call this character The Warlock. The Heroine takes care of him the way he deserves.

## The Big Guy

Every story has a Big Guy; Han Solo has Chewbacca; Dumbledore has Hagrid; Morpheus has Dozer; Professor X has Colossus; The Avengers have the Hulk. The defining powers of The Big Guy are, of course, size and strength. He can be good or bad; many stories have one of each.

Big guys represent unbound, primal emotions. They are not very brilliant because emotion and intelligence lie on opposite ends of the psyche. For that reason, though, they make good sidekicks.

**Good Big Guys** show innocent, almost child-like qualities.

Examples:

> In ***Star Wars,*** Han Solo warns everybody that Chewbacca better win at holographic chess because Wookies tend to rip off their opponent's arms when they lose.
>
> In ***Deadpool*** (2016), Colossus averts his eyes from Angel Dust's (Gina Carano) because one of her breasts was left exposed during the fight. She takes advantage of his infantile reaction and punches the chromed giant right in the crotch.

***Hellboy*** (2014) is a curious case of a Big Guy who's also the Hero. He is immature for his age. (Also, note the word 'boy' in his name.)

A failed use of the archetype of the Big Guy is found in *Green Lantern,* (2011): Kilowog is supposed to be a good guy, both he's both pedantic and gratuitously violent, two characteristics that don't match the profile of a good Big Guy.

Bad Big Guys represent unbound and primal emotions, too, albeit negative ones. The bad Big Guy is unrepentantly violent in a big, hairy, and ugly version. His weak spot is his stupidity, so he is usually defeated by using his strength against himself.

Examples:

> ***Star Wars*** (Episode VI - 1983): Luke lures the monstrous Rancor into following him, and then he closes the iron gate of the monster's own dungeon on its head.
>
> ***The Lord of the Rings:*** Gandalf lures the Balrog into following him through a thin, long stone bridge, which Gandalf timely breaks with his staff, so the bridge collapses under the monster's own weight.
>
> ***Harry Potter:*** The mountain troll is knocked out by Ron by performing a *Wingardium Leviosa* spell that makes the troll's own club fall on its head.

Big guys and giants in general (especially if they are bad) are associated with fire because volcanoes, fires, and lightning are natural forces that man cannot tame. Examples are the Balrog, Surtur (from *Thor: Ragnarok,* 2017), and Hellboy.

Stones are also a usual association for giants because of mountains (big and made of stone) and because stones are what magma (fire) eventually turns into. Examples: The Basilisk (which petrifies with its eyes), the giants of stone fighting in the mountains in The Hobbit, the character The Thing in the Fantastic Four (2015), and so on.

## The Little Guy

The Little Guy (he's almost always male) is annoying, clumsy, and somewhat of a twerp. That makes him an excellent candidate to play the roles of the Comic Relief or The Fool (described below).

Do not associate being small with being all those things, though. Many physically small characters have crucial roles and immense courage, like Frodo, R2D2, Yoda, BB-8, Gimli, Ant-Man, and many more.

If the evil team has a Little Guy, he is definitely a male, and he is definitely "little" also in a human sense: A cowardly, sycophantic little person. Examples: Wormtongue (from *The Lord of The Rings* series), Alfrid Lickspittle (*The Hobbit* series), and Peter Pettigrew (*Harry Potter* series).

# 8. Character Functions

*This song has already been written*
*up to the last detail*
*Everything is a lie, you'll see*
*Poetry is the only truth.*

(*Déjà Vu,* Music and lyrics by Gustavo Cerati)

**J**ames Bond is not the most complex of blokes. Granted, he is a spy, a martial artist, a playboy, a commander in the British Secret Service, and he is unbeatable at baccarat, poker, or any other aristocratic game you can think of. However, that doesn't tell us a lot about his personality.

Without leaving the spy genre, we have a more complex character in the humble Benji Dunn (Simon Pegg) from *Mission: Impossible.* Benji is Ethan Hunt's sidekick, but he is also The Geek, The Comedic Relief, and sometimes he acts as The Fool, too (all roles discussed in this chapter).

Note how *complexity* is not a matter of backstory: We know nothing about the past of either of them. The thing is, James Bond has a list of abilities, while Benji Dunn has a list of functions. The more functions a character plays, the more interesting it becomes.

So, what are these functions? Let's see them in detail. Remember: these are not characters, but character *functions,* which can be performed by some fitting character taken from the list in the previous chapter.

## The Reluctant Helper

The Reluctant Helper is critical to the success of a quest, but this character is not part of the good guys' team. Actually, he's not part of any team. The Reluctant Helper remains reclusive, seemingly unaffected by any worldly problems. He (or she) is beyond good and evil.

The Reluctant Helper is usually cynical and individualistic and always demands something in exchange for their services.

Examples:

> **Star Wars:** In *The Phantom Menace,* Watto, who owns Anakin and his mother as slaves, will let the kid go in exchange for the money prize of the pod race.
>
> **Harry Potter:** The ghost of Helena Ravenclaw reveals the location of her mother's diadem only after Harry swears to destroy the cursed object.
>
> In **The Matrix Reloaded,** Persephone will only help if Neo gives her one true kiss. It makes sense: In a simulated world, where everything has been already written up to the last detail, everything is a lie— feelings are the only truth.

Note that I am not calling this character an "ally" but a "helper" because their intervention is just a one-time thing. In the few cases in which this character stays with the team, they usually become a Traitor. Example: D.J. (Benicio Del Toro, in *Star Wars: The Last Jedi).* His philosophy of life is *"It's all a machine, partner. Live free, don't join."* He stays with Finn and Rose and eventually betrays them. This is a Reluctant Helper acting as a Traitor.

## The Traitor

Traitors are good examples of what a character's *function* is, as opposed to a character's *role.* Traitors are necessary because they move the story forward by triggering the Evil Twist (explained in Chapter 11). Traitors are usually minor characters because they must go unnoticed. We know that something about them is not right, but we can't put our finger on it. That's why we disregard them. And then... *BAM!* They hit in the worst possible moment: When the good guys needed him the most.

Example: Cypher, from *The Matrix*. He is just a creep hovering in there, stalking Trinity, seeding doubt in Neo's mind, and playing dumb. And then he kills everyone.

The Traitor secretly works for the dark side, but unlike the Witch, he doesn't do it because of sadistic pleasure. No: The Traitor does it for money and revenge. Cypher, for example, wants to punish Morpheus. Also, as payment for his betrayal, he demands to be reconnected to The Matrix as a rich and famous man.

Also, the traitors act out of romantic resentment: They realize that the person they desire (Cypher desires Trinity, Grima Wormtongue desires Éowin) will never be theirs.

Why does the Traitor's move ultimately fail? Because they underestimate the Hero's talent. They fail, and they die; whatever 'death' means in the context of a particular story, a traitor must die—full stop. And who delivers the karma? The Sidekick does.

Examples:

> ***The Matrix:*** Cypher left Tank for dead. Big mistake. Tank fries Cypher with the same lightning rifle the traitor used to kill the others.
>
> ***Harry Potter:*** Peter Pettigrew keeps the boys as prisoners in Malfoy Manor's cellar. Dobby shoots him in the back.
>
> ***The Lord of The Rings:*** Grima Wormtongue, who betrayed King Théoden, stabs his new master Saruman in the back. Legolas (a sidekick in this story) kills him with an arrow.
>
> ***Aliens:*** Burke is not killed by the Sidekick (which in this story should be the android Bishop), but by the very creatures he set out to harvest. A traitor's death is more cathartic if it has a touch of irony.

Stories usually have either a Traitor or a False Ally, but not both, because their functions are similar, if not the same. Exception: Complex works with parallel lines, like *The Lord of the Rings* saga, where Wormtongue is a traitor and Gollum is a false ally.

## The Infiltrated agent

Spies work in secret; they aren't a traitor working for the enemy—they *are* the enemy. Note that the Agent can be a bad guy or a good guy, depending on what team they are secretly working for. If he's working for our team, we call him a patriot.

## The Circumstantial Ally

The Circumstantial Ally is a declared enemy whom the Good Guys must join forces with to defeat a bigger threat. Example from history: the USA and the USSR during World War II. Circumstantial allies introduce interest and complexity in a story's theme.

## The Odd Ally

There is something strange about the Odd Ally. They aren't necessarily creepy or anything, but there's something that keeps them apart from traditional society. The Hero makes friends with this secluded character, and it is precisely that proximity that motivates the Odd Ally to help the Hero.

How does the Hero come in contact with the Odd Ally? By entering their territory. The journey takes our protagonist through odd places, and that's where odd people are.

*In Home Alone 2 – Lost in New York* (1992), the odd ally is the Pigeon Lady, a homeless woman whom Kevin befriends in Central Park. During the climax of the movie, Pigeon Lady comes to Kevin's rescue, dousing the grease-covered bandits in birdseed; her flock descends and pecks them into submission. Other:

> **Star Wars:** The Ewoks push the Battle of Endor in favor of the Rebellion. The fight is taking place in their backyard, after all.
>
> **Harry Potter** makes lots of odd friends in odd places: Buckbeak the Hippogriff (in the Magic Forest where it lives), the ghost of Moaning Myrtle (in the Bathroom where she "lives"), and so on.

In ***The Matrix,*** the Odd Ally is Spoon Boy. "There is no spoon," the kid says. His words return during the scene in which Neo realizes that he is indeed The One.

## The Comedic Relief

I am convinced that a touch of humor is always necessary, no matter the genre. Humor tells the audience: "Remember, this is supposed to be entertaining," even in drama or horror stories. One funny word or gesture can ease the unbearable tension of some scenes.

Whatever the character in charge of these light touches, they act as the Comedic Relief. The lighter the genre, the more characters get in and out of this role.

Examples:

> In ***Star Wars,*** the comedic reliefs are Han Solo (occasionally), C-3PO (frequently), and sometimes R2D2 and Chewbacca, who make us smile without ever pronouncing an intelligible word.
>
> In ***The Matrix,*** there are only one or two barely humorous lines. The Matrix is my all-time favorite movie, but I think that it takes itself a bit too seriously.
>
> In ***Harry Potter,*** the comedic relief is Ron Weasley. Neville Longbottom, in turn, usually plays the role of the Fool or the Innocent, but he also has some comedic moments.

Remember: We are talking about a touch of humor, and the more serious the story, the lighter the touch should be. A perplexed look, a funny reaction, or a dorky movement might suffice.

## The Geek

The Geek (usually a male, but never an overly masculine character) is the technological genius that supports the Hero and the rest of the team. In many stories, this function is carried by the Sidekick because whoever acts as The Geek has to be entirely dependable. The Geek is also in charge of the info-dumps: He explains how things work and what the plan is.

Examples of characters in The Geek role are Scotty in *Star Trek,*

"Q" in James Bond movies, R2D2 in *Star Wars* (he opens all the locks and repairs all the malfunctions), Tank in *The Matrix*, and the already mentioned Benji Dunn *(Mission: Impossible).*

## The Fool

A court's fool (also called a buffoon, a trickster, or a jester) counterbalanced the king's narcissism by candidly exposing truths by means of sarcasm and ridicule. The fool could make jokes about his majesty that would send anyone else to an appointment with the executioner.

We find these tricksters in our lives, too: Bigmouths, pranksters, older people, little children... People who embarrass us in front of others with a joke or a misplaced remark. Whenever it happens to me, I try to transcend my irritation and see how they are pointing out a truth that I somehow denied. (Not that I actively pursue their company, of course.)

In a story, the function of the Fool (which is almost always carried out by the Little Guy—explained above) has several characteristics:

**The Fool needs to explain everything,** providing an opportunity for the audience to understand what's going on.

**The Fool is a bigmouth,** propagating information among the characters. His indiscretion creates conflict or triggers epiphanies, both things that keep a story moving. The Fool gets reprimanded, anyway.

**The Fool complicates things** with his physical clumsiness, too.

**The Fool shows the humanity of the Hero.** While all characters shun him or reprimand him, the Fool is treated by the Hero with tolerance and kindness.

In our example movies, the fools are:

> In ***Star Wars,*** Jar Jar Binks, who conducts himself like a clown. He gets reprimanded by the Gungan leader.
>
> In ***The Matrix,*** the fool is Mouse. During lunch, in front of everyone, he offers Neo a "much more personalized meeting" with the Woman in the Red Dress. He gets shunned.

In **Harry Potter,** the bigmouth is Hagrid. *"I shouldn't have said that. I should not have said that!"* he reprimands himself. Other characters also step in and out of the Fool's role: Neville Longbottom, Seamus Finnigan, and Dobby The Elf.

In ***The Lord of the Rings,*** the fool is Pippin (Billy Boyd). "Fool of a Took!" Gandalf reprimands him when Pippin accidentally drops a bucket down a dry well, waking up every last Goblin in the mines of Moria.

## The Innocent

In storytelling, we find two kinds of Innocent.

**The Awkward Innocent** is usually a rookie who's trying to fit in the team, someone who points out the truth too candidly. Just like the Fool, the Innocent is often a young person, thin, small, and in many stories is also the Comedic Relief.

**The Oblivious Innocent** (usually a female character, like an old lady) is someone oblivious to what's going on, someone going about her daily business, blind to the fight between good and evil.

For example, in *Harry Potter,* Ron, Hermione, and Harry are sitting at a coffee bar when two Death Eaters try to kill them. A terrible shooting starts. The waitress, working back in the kitchen, listens to music with her headphones on, totally ignorant of the violent fight happening a few feet away.

## The Romantic Interest

Romantic subplots are the most typical path to the symbolic union at the end of a story; that's why romance fits in many genres. The Romantic interest is a function typically performed by the Hero (or the Heroine) and the Goddess (or the Prince Charming).

At first, things are never easy for the turtledoves, though.

Examples:

> In ***Star Wars,*** Han says to Leia: *"Look, 'Your Worshipfulness,' let's get one thing straight: I take orders from just one person—me!"* And she says: *"You stuck-up, half-witted, scruffy-looking*

*nerf herder!"*

The **Harry Potter** saga only approaches romance in the later movies, once the kids have reached puberty. In the meantime, Hermione treats Ron with some disdain, and Ron says of her: *"Mental, that one. I'm telling you."*

In **The Matrix,** Neo tells Trinity: *"The Trinity? The one that cracked the IRS database? I thought you were a guy."* She treats him like a basic dude by answering, *"Most guys do."* And eventually, she will tell him to go to hell, too.

Things improve for them, romantically speaking, as soon as they fight arm-in-arm. (See Hero/Goddess dynamics on page 102).

## The Temptress

We need to be careful with stereotypes here. I refer to this character as if it were female, but it can also be male, or even some other kind of temptation of an erotic or materialistic nature.

The Temptress doesn't necessarily want to hurt the Hero (like the Witch does); in storytelling, the Temptress represents the Ordinary World trying to divert the Hero from his path. In psychological terms, the Temptress is a hysteric person (in Freudian terms) teasing others into a trap, luring them with their seductive aura, but never delivering the goods.

The typical Temptress' traits are (both in movies and real life):

**They are impacting at first sight,** which may make them look like goddesses. They're not.

**It all looks like a match made in heaven.** You discover in a few minutes that you have so much in common with them that you start looking for a chapel.

**They become the subject of the conversation.** Soon enough, most of the Temptress sentences become full of *I's* and *me's*.

**The relationship advances rapidly.** And it will quickly derail, as well.

**Temptresses demand constant attention.** They feel hot, they feel cold, they are hungry, they are not hungry anymore, and so all day long.

**There's no way to satisfy them.** Ignore their complaints, and they get angry; satisfy their complaints, and they get bored.

**They look too good to be true.** How come is this attractive, charming person alone? Well, read this list again.

*Does the Hero fall for the temptation?*

Nope. The objective of the encounter is to show the Hero's willpower. He either ignores the seduction or negotiates a compromise. Examples:

> **Star Wars:** Two beautiful girls (the Tonnika sisters) stare at Luke when he enters the Cantina in Mos Eisley, luring him with their gaze. He ignores them and walks away, following Obi-Wan. (The whole scene lasts about 2 seconds).
>
> In **Harry Potter,** temptation shows up in the form of a lady carrying a cart full of sweets. Ron rejects the offer. Harry, however, buys the lot. Oh, well—the poor kid probably never tasted candy before.
>
> In **The Matrix,** the attractive Dujour (the girl with the White Rabbit tattoo) tempts Neo into going to a party by using sexual innuendo. Neo rejects the offer. However, he accepts as soon as he understands Trinity's message (*"Follow the White Rabbit"*).

*Ghostbusters* (1984) shows a rare case of a goddess in a temptress function. Dr. Peter Venkman (Bill Murray) is in love with Dana Barrett (Sigourney Weaver). She, possessed by a demon (example of a woman "in the *animus"),* provokes him, saying, *"I want you inside me."* Peter declines: *"No. It sounds like you've got at least two people in there already."*

## The Rational Wimp

The Rational Wimp is a character dominated by an overly rational aspect of the psyche. He (usually a male character) has learned to lean heavily on his thinking, denying his emotional side. Thus, unable to control his emotions, he inadequately communicates with others.

Why do I use the word "wimp" to describe this function? Because this character is frightful, always forewarning of impending catastrophes. He is irritating, so he frequently gets shushed.

The proper function of the Rational Wimp is to remind the audience of the severity of the situation in a particular scene and how high the stakes are.

The classic example of a Rational Wimp is C-3PO. *"Sir, the possibility of successfully navigating an asteroid field is approximately 3,720 to 1,"* he says. *"Never tell me the odds!"* Han Solo reprimands him. Ironically, C-3PO is fluent in 6 million forms of communication, but his communication style irritates everyone. R2D2 is the opposite of a Rational Wimp: The little droid doesn't say a word and delivers.

## The Gatekeepers

Each gate needs a Gatekeeper.

Depending on the genre and the situation, the gatekeeper can be a security guard, a Doberman, a fire-spitting dragon, or the lady at the DMV counter. It can also be a password, a magic lock, or a lazy cat in front of the bathroom door, sleeping belly-up on yesterday's underwear. Entering the setting of a new scene, the physical place where the next actions will develop must always imply sorting some kind of an obstacle.

Gatekeepers (in my book *The Ultimate Hero's Journey* I call "Guardians") show that advancing through the adventure has a cost. They also allow the protagonists to show off their talents and personalities as they solve the obstructions in different ways.

## The Herald

I left the function of the Herald for the end of this chapter because it stands at the center of many scenes. This is The Herald's arc, which must intertwine with the regular arc of whatever character is fulfilling this Herald function:

**1) The Herald awaits for the right moment. Secrecy is necessary to avoid alerting the dark side and the hero's Sur-**

rogate Parents.

> **R2D2** waits until night time to go looking for Obi-Wan.
> **Trinity** waits for the right moment to contact Neo.
> **Hundreds of owls** wait for Harry outside the Dursley's home.

## 2) The herald delivers a first message, which soon vanishes.

> **R2D2** projects a holographic message, which soon disappears.
> **Trinity** messages Neo on his PC. *"Wake up, Neo."* It disappears.
> **Dumbledore** sends Harry a letter. Uncle Vernon destroys it.
> ***Mission Impossible*** offers the most iconic instance of this stage:
> "This message will self-destruct in five seconds."

## 3) The Herald delivers a second message. Then the Herald vanishes.

> **R2D2** disappears after projecting the hologram.
> **Trinity** disappears after meeting Neo in a disco.
> **Hagrid** literally disappears after giving Harry his train ticket.

## 4) The Herald returns: The Herald comes and goes in order to evade the dark side. They have to move fast.

> **R2D2** reappears in the rock canyon. Luke instructs C-3PO to move fast.
> **Trinity** reappears and tells Neo to get in the car. They have to move fast.
> **Hagrid** reappears at Hogsmeade's station. He tells the kids to move fast.

## 5) The Herald ride: Using a vehicle, the Herald takes the Hero to the first meeting with the Mentor. Both the route and the vehicle are memorable.

> **C-3PO** (in a herald's function) drives a floating speeder through the desert.
> **Trinity** takes Neo to Morpheus in a 1965 Lincoln Continental.
> **Hagrid** takes the kids to the castle on magical boats.

## 6) The Herald delivers a gift: It can be an object, or information, or some advice.

> **R2D2** plays the holographic message in full, in front of Luke.
> **Trinity** offers Neo a piece of advice regarding Morpheus: *"Be*

*honest. He knows more that you can imagine."*
**Hagrid** brings Harry a birthday gift: Hedwig the Owl.

## 7) The Herald witnesses the introductions and then leaves. Time is of the essence.

*Star Wars:* Ben introduces himself as Obi-Wan. They have to leave the canyon quickly. Once in the cave, **C-3PO** asks for permission to close down for a while (i.e., he "leaves" them).

*The Matrix:* Morpheus introduces himself. He says, *"I don't know if you are ready to see what I want to show you, but sadly, you and I have run out of time."* **Trinity** leaves.

*Harry Potter:* **Professor McGonagall** (in a Herald's role) prepares the newcomers to meet Dumbledore in the Grand Hall "momentarily" (time pressure). Once the kids are introduced and sorted into the four houses, she leaves the scene.

To end this chapter, let me note that some of the functions that we analyzed are mutually incompatible. Heralds are a good example: they are dedicated soldiers of the light side, so if your story has a Herald function, they cannot be the traitor.

Also, the functions discussed above are intended to give depth to minor characters, not the big four (the Villain, the Hero, the Goddess, the Mentor). True, sometimes the Hero himself plays the Fool, but only in comedies, like *Johnny English* (2003) and *Zoolander* (2001), or in dramedies, like *Forrest Gump* (1994). In any other genre, making the Hero a fool will create an archetypal short-circuit.

# 9. Character Dynamics

> *"We've got a blind date with destiny, and it looks like she's ordered the lobster."*
>
> (*Mystery Men,* 1999).

**P**hilosopher Slavoj Žižek wants me to tell you something dirty about me. He says:

> Real human contact is very difficult to achieve unless there's a small exchange of obscenities said in such a way that we just laugh, and the more we tell them, the more we are friends.[14]

Theater master Keith Johnstone agrees:

> If you can make the students playfully insult each other, then work becomes easier. Even the most rigid, self-conscious, and defensive people suddenly unbend.[15]

I don't know if women bond this way; my wife and my female friends tell me that they don't: Women bond through empathy, like a sisterhood. But I'm a dude, so the obscenity thing works in my case.

---

*14 - On Political Correctness: Why "Tolerance" Is Patronizing – YouTube, https://rebrand.ly/bef1b. (Edited for clarity and to remove the original context related to post-racism.)*

*15 - Impro - Improvisation and the theater, Methuen Drama, 2007 - p. 53 (edited for clarity).*

So this is my dirty secret for you: When I meet a good friend, I greet them warmly and exchange niceties, but when I meet my best friend, or when I meet my little brother, I scold them for not having called me sooner, accusing them of having been too busy giving five-dollar fellatios to muscular, tattooed sailors in some god-forsaken back alley. They immediately accuse me of something worse (two-dollar fellatios are a classic), and then we fuse in a big hug, immensely happy to see each other again. We are then free to talk about whatever we want.

A dialog between friends is playful; it is a status game as well, but it raises and lowers rhythmically, like in a see-saw. A friend is a person with whom we have an unspoken agreement to play friendly status games.[16]

*Nice story. Now, how does it relate to character design?*

It relates to character dynamics. Back in Chapter 1, we said that stories are about freedom and about finding a home. And as it turns out, both those things have to do with status.

*Why with 'status'?*

Because without status, there's no freedom, and without freedom, there's no home. And good stories end up wherever the hero calls *home.*

I believe that confrontational dialog is the most interesting kind of dialog, and in a novel, all dialog should be confrontational at some level, even subtly so. A dialog without any "status skirmishes" is boring. It's like fencing: Words are stockades, and retractions are strategic regroupings. Or like poker, where characters play or hold dialectical cards, so revealing their personalities.

Especially interesting is the dialog between two characters with very different statuses, like during an interrogation, for example. The interrogator has plenty of power, and the interrogated person is detained against their will. Will she lie, or will she tell the truth? What if the exchange was between a Duchess and a drunk vagabond? How would a lady react to the delirious fantasies and lack of protocol of a disheveled character?

---

16 - Impro - Improvisation and the theater, Methuen Drama, 2007 - p. 53 (edited for clarity).

Important: The dialectical status game is not about winning more status, nor about proving oneself more valuable than the other person. The object of the game is to *obtain* something. All stories are epics, and all epics are quests.

In the sections below, we will analyze the status relations between the Big Four, taken in pairs.

## Dynamics Hero/Hero

The role of the Hero is sometimes shared by two characters (or more), so the dynamics between them are especially important.

In **Star Trek,** for example, Spock is not Kirk's sidekick but more like a "co-hero" because of their complementarity. Spock is wise and rational; Kirk is bold and creative. Spock thinks; Kirk thinks out of the box. They are so symbiotic that they represent one single ego.

**The Three Stooges** and **The Three Amigos** are rare instances of three characters with the same role and the same protagonism, which I think can only work in comedies. **The Three Musketeers,** instead, is a triple mentor role, with young D'Artagnan as the Hero.

I don't remember any stories with quadruple heroes. I wonder if there is any. A Beatles biopic, maybe?

## Dynamics Hero/Villain

Heroes and villains share a common origin, to the point that the Villain's resentment and the Hero's trauma usually come from the same event. Examples:

> **Star Wars:** Vader and Luke were "born" from the same tragedy: Padmé's death.
>
> **The Matrix:** Humans created the Machines, and the Machines created a human to solve the inherent imbalance in The Matrix.
>
> **Harry Potter:** Harry's resilience and Voldemort's exile have a common origin: Lilly Potter's death.
>
> In **Batman** (1989), Jack Napier "created" Batman when he killed Bruce Wayne's parents, and The Joker was created

when Jack Napier fell into a pool full of chemicals during a fight with... Batman.

***Austin Powers*** (1997) parodies the common origin thing: Austin and Dr. Evil are twins who were separated as babies when their mother died in a car explosion.

The Hero and Villain dynamics create mirrored arcs (see graphic on pages 48 and 50). Being opposing forces, when one goes up, the other goes down, and vice versa. Example: Mr. Incredible *(The Incredibles,* 2004) falls from hero to zero, while Syndrome ascends from zero to supervillain. And then the paths invert and mirror each other again, up until the final, unavoidable clash.

## Dynamics Hero/Goddess

The connection that the Hero and Goddess share doesn't have to be romantic, but it usually is, opening the romantic subplot of the story. We know that the goddess lost someone (often a positive male figure, typically her father) and that the Hero lost a female figure, so they both represent the contrasexual figure that the other one is missing. Their backstories foreshadow their final unification.

The paths of the Hero and the Goddess run parallel (see the converging and parallel paths of Cinderella and Prince Charming, on page 48). Still, they do it "back-to-back" in terms of the way they interact with reality: The ego looks outward to the external world, and the anima looks inward to the inner world. The ego is more intellectual; the anima is more instinctual. If they were looking at the world in the same way, thinking and reacting in the same way, we wouldn't need the two of them.

What is more, the relationship between Hero and Goddess is not only complementary but also compensatory: Only when the Hero shows what he's made of can the Goddess return to femininity. Our psychic lives are not too different; the more socially compliant the ego pretends to be (via the persona), the more instinctual, primitive, and belligerent the anima becomes.

Mythically, masculine and feminine principles tend to integration. Such a broad statement is not true for every story nor every character, of course, but it makes evolutive sense; after all, that's how babies are made. On a deeper level, it makes symbolic sense, too: An allegory of the integration of the soul-image (anima or animus) into one's consciousness.

Brief detour here: The union of the ego and the anima is not necessarily good advice for real life. Von Franz points out that marrying a person on whom one has projected one's own anima/animus is a recipe for disaster.[17] Traditional tales show it, too: Each time a male falls in love with a sort of mythological feminine figure, in the end, she disappears (the mermaid returns to the sea, or a girl converted into a bird flies away). At risk of being repetitive, let me say that Hero and Goddess are not each other's soul-image, but *the story's* soul-images. Their union is a symbol of the story (the psyche) becoming whole by integrating its component archetypes.

## Dynamics Mentor/Villain

The Mentor can't defeat the Villain, and he knows it; he only fights to enable the Hero to keep fighting.

The bad news is that the Mentor will not make it through.

The sacrifice of the Mentor, however, transfers power to the Hero, but how that works is never clear. Examples:

> ***Star Wars:*** Obi-Wan's sacrifice transfers his Force to Luke, somehow.
>
> ***The Matrix:*** Morpheus' sacrifice forces Neo to make a choice.
>
> ***Harry Potter:*** Dumbledore allows Draco to disarm him, and then he begs Snape to kill him. This transfers the power of the Elder Wand to Harry by means of the intricate workings of the magical object's allegiance.

## Dynamics Hero/Mentor

The Mentor's path was always meant to diverge from the Hero's. But there is a psychological divergence as well because the

---

17 - Marie-Louise von Franz, Animus and Anima in Fairy Tales - Inner City Books, 2002 – p.58.

Hero has to dis-identify with the Mentor. Why "dis-identify"? Because in order to become his own man, a man has to liberate himself from his father, either the biological one, the symbolic one, or both.[18] This separation happens when the Hero discovers the Mentor's rather manipulative ways. Examples:

> **Star Wars:** Luke realizes that his father wasn't killed by Vader as Obi-Wan told him.
>
> **The Matrix:** Neo thinks that Morpheus is wrong about the Prophecy, and he resents Morpheus because now he can't go back, either Neo wants it or not.
>
> **Harry Potter:** Harry eventually understands that Dumbledore is actually prepping him to act as a weapon, and that he will be sacrificed.

Such realizations break the Hero's fascination with the Mentor, enabling the Hero to take matters into his own hands. Examples:

> **Star Wars:** Luke devises a new plan despite what Obi-Wan and Yoda say. He will use his father's inner conflict to bring him back from the Dark Side.
>
> **The Matrix:** Neo devises a new plan despite what Morpheus said *("Neo must get out; he's the only thing that matters")*. Neo will attempt to rescue Morpheus to save both him and Zion.
>
> **Harry Potter**'s disenchantment with Dumbledore is palpable: A moment arrives in the saga in which Harry stops smiling altogether. But he decisively takes the lead in the fight.

## Dynamics Mentor/Grand-Villain

This fight rarely happens, but if it does, it ends in a stalemate. Example: Yoda (a sort of Grand-mentor) confronts Darth Sidious (Grand-Villain). Sidious escapes, and no one wins.

*So, there's no way to defeat the Grand-villain?*

Not for the Mentor. Grand Villains can be defeated only by:

---

18 - J. Jacobi, *The Psychology of C.G. Jung* - p.126

1) The Hero, of course.

2) The Villain himself, either out of repentance (In *Star Wars*, Vader kills Darth Sidious) or out of ambition (Kylo Ren kills Supreme Leader Snoke).

## Dynamics Goddess/Mentor

The Goddess is not a very social person. Life has been hard for her, and she trusts nobody except the Mentor. Examples:

> ***Star Wars:*** Leia sends the holographic message to the only person she can trust—Obi-Wan.
>
> ***The Matrix:*** Trinity is the second in rank in the ship and Morpheus's right hand.
>
> ***Harry Potter:*** Hermione creates "Dumbledore's Army." Also, note that she doesn't have any female friends.

## Dynamics Goddess/Villain

The Villain had to have some role in the original damage inflicted on the Goddess; that's why she's looking for payback. The Goddess, however, cannot defeat the Villain alone. That's the Hero's (or the Heroine's) job.

The Goddess doesn't directly fight the Witch, either. The Goddess fights both the Henchmen and the Warlock.

She wins.

## Dynamics Goddess/Oracle (or the lack of it)

One could think that the two principal female characters should naturally have a sort of mother-daughter dynamic, but it doesn't happen (at least not in male-centric stories).

Examples:

> ***Star Wars:*** Leia's has two motherly figures, Padmé Amidala and Breha Organa. We see nothing about those relationships.
>
> ***The Matrix:*** the Oracle made Trinity a critical prediction, but that happens off-screen. When we finally see them together, they behave as if they were strangers.

***Harry Potter:*** The relationship between Hermione and adoptive motherly figures, like McGonagall or other female professors, is not explored at all.

I believe that the Goddess and the Oracle, being both feminine and positive energies, keep each other at a distance. There is no conflict that could make them interact. This disconnection doesn't apply to Heroines, of course. Heroines must receive The Prophecy from the Oracle, just like Heroes do.

This reminds me of something called "the Bechdel test." It checks whether a work of fiction features at least one instance of two female characters talking about something other than a man. Surprisingly, few works of fiction pass it.

(By the way, my own fiction works do pass the Bechdel test, but barely.)

# 10. Creating Deep Characters

> *"You got a nice suit at home, or do you like coming to work every day dressed like you're goin' to invade Poland?"*
>
> (From *The Departed*, 2006)

**H**eather is the girl from work who eats burgers and wings but has the body of a salad girl.

In a Saturday Night Live skit, comedian Cecily Strong interprets a "one-dimensional female character from a male-driven comedy." She's interviewed so she can give her opinion on the underrepresentation of women in major film roles.[19]

*"Hi, I'm Heather, from work. You probably haven't noticed me because I wear glasses. But later, I might take them off, and you might notice me."*

She keeps stating rhetorical commonplaces without ever getting to any point. So, how do we design characters that feel like real people (i.e., not "one-dimensional")?

In order not to be as superficial as Heather, a character should have the following dimensions:[20]

---

*19 - SNL Weekend Update: One Dimensional Female – YouTube: https://rebrand.ly/15861*
*20 - Lajos Egri, The Art of Dramatic Writing – BN Publishing, 2009.*

**A physical dimension:** Height, weight, ethnic background, hair color, gender, etc.

**A social dimension:** Class, origins, upbringing, religion, studies, profession, etc.

**A psychological dimension:** Talent, weakness, objectives, mood, personality, etc.

Don't exaggerate with the descriptions, though, because readers like to visualize characters for themselves. (Also, some would argue that listing abundant personal characteristics it's not very good writing form).

Okay, let's simplify this another notch: For each character, you must define how they look, what they want, and what they are good at. And then you will have to put them to play status games, each of them trying to obtain what they want or need.

Those requirements are useful to describe a character that aspires to feel real. However, it is not necessary, and certainly not sufficient. So, let's see what other resources we have to give characters life-like depth.

## A Hero that audiences will love

Arthur Conan Doyle was clever: He made Watson the point-of-view character—not Sherlock. John Watson is a "normal" person; Sherlock Holmes is a borderline sociopath. His intellectual power is so great that it risks being unrelatable, but we can approach him through his inseparable sidekick, the brave, good doctor.

'Relatable' is the keyword.

*So, what makes a Hero relatable?*

Relatable heroes do the following:

**Relatable Heroes ask the questions the audience is asking.** Chief among them is, "What the hell is going on?"

**Relatable Heroes care for the weak and the innocent.** In a world overtaken by evil, selfishness is on the rise. But the Hero stops for a moment and tends to someone in trouble, showing his sensibility. Example: Mr. Incredible (*The Incredi-*

*bles,* 2004) stops chasing some vicious criminals to help an old lady bring down her kitty from a huge tree. And then he smashes the bad guys' car with that tree.

**Relatable Heroes allow the audience inside their minds.** We understand Sherlock because he explains his incredible deductions to Watson, and we understand Dexter because we can hear his thoughts.

**Relatable Heroes feel fear.** We all do; we can relate to that. But remember: no cowardly heroes. He can be a bit wimpy for comedic effect, but only at the beginning of the story.

**Relatable Heroes introduce a touch of humor.** (Described back on page 91).

Allow the audience to root for your Hero or Heroine; keep them real and human (or "humane", I could say), no matter if your story is about Pandorians, Pokémons, or Power Rangers.

## Subverting stereotypes

Imagine that your female protagonist's best friend (her sidekick) is a gay man—a classic in romantic comedies. If you fit this man into a stereotype, you might describe him as handsome, flirty, owner of an aesthetic sensibility, a flair for fashion, and a joyful disposition. We have seen that character so many times.

But what if this person, in addition to being gay, were also a masculine, hairy, six-foot-six tall man with a fourth-degree karate black belt? What if he couldn't shop for clothes on his own because he's colorblind and consistently picks out jarring shades of orange and violet? Now some exciting possibilities just opened up. And I was toying with the physical dimension only; to fully understand a character, we must uncover their desires and motives. So, let's see even more ways to give a character depth as a story progresses.

## Depth by contradiction

Inherent contradictions can make a character unforgettable. The Wizard of Oz, for example, has a cowardly Lion, a Good Witch, a girl who already has what she is looking for, a robot with more feelings than a human, and a Scarecrow who only knows that he knows nothing—and so he achieves wisdom.

Sadly, I can't elaborate much because there's no way to discuss this topic in general terms: The contradiction has to be something individual, something at the core of a character's personality, and only the author is in control of that. But I can say this: A good contradiction should be an ironic one, either relating to both a character's weakness and their talent.

## Depth by quirks

Robert Langdon, the protagonist of Dan Brown's novels (*The Da Vinci Code, Angels and Demons,* and others), has a talent: He is a professor of Art History specialized in symbology. Yeah, not a very exciting job for the protagonist of a fast-paced thriller.

No, seriously. Langdon is boring. He is a middle-aged, middle-class, middle-everything character whose weirdest trait is that he wears a Mickey Mouse wristwatch. Even his claustrophobia is not a real weakness but only a mild inconvenience during elevator rides. If only that claustrophobia were a symptom of his unconscious feeling of "being trapped in the closet," that would be mildly interesting. Alas, no such luck. Even Brown laughed about it: When Langdon arrives in The Vatican to solve a crisis involving an antimatter bomb, the commander of the Swiss Guard says, *"What a relief—the symbologist is here."*

And what's up with the goddesses in Dan Brown's novels? They are always long-haired, hot-looking, bright, brunette scientists with no quirkiness or backstories at all. I imagine them like one of those shopping-mall L'Oréal cardboard cutouts.

A character's quirkiness is not central to the plot; the Talent and the Trauma are. But some whimsical, contra-stereotypical, and even dirty touches (like Slavoj Žižek recommended) can make an audience feel like they're friends with your character. Say, for example, that the mentor is an Italian guy who eats pizza only if it comes with a pineapple topping in a way that's meaningful somehow. Trust me, I'm Italian; for me, pizza with pineapple topping qualifies as one of the capital sins. But do it well, and your characters may feel pretty human with just a couple of little silly touches.

## A dangerous move: Depth by role-reversal

Isn't it great when a villain is unmasked at the end, á la Hercule Poirot? Such is the essence of whodunit movies and good detective novels. However, I hate it when the "hero" turns out to be the bad guy in the end.

Swapping roles in the middle of a story could be surprising, but it could also make your audience feel betrayed because it destroys the identifications they formed along the narration. And it is not very original, either: It has been done, many times. I have forgotten the name of those stories.

Consider leaving such reversals for minor characters only: The False Enemy, the False Ally, and the Traitor of your story. They will provide all the surprise the story needs and won't risk alienating the reader. But of course, it is up to you.

## Another tricky one: Depth by backstory

Giving depth to a character means revealing their backstory gradually. But beware: Audiences enjoy witnessing present reactions, not ancient anecdotes—the proverbial "show, don't tell." The author must find an interesting way to summon the resentments, traumas, and losses of all characters, coming through the echoes of old wounds that still hurt, all without writing a boring biography in the process.

## Depth by a change of names

American philosopher Ken Wilber defines evolution "as a process of inclusion and transcendence": You outgrow your old self, but you take it with you for the ride.[21]

Characters, particularly the hero and the villain, as they progress through the story, they evolve. Two evident signs of their evo-

---

*21 - Ken Wilber, A Brief History of Everything - Shambala, 2001.*

lution are changes in appearance and changes in their names, because their names or titles show their relative status at each point. Examples:

> **Star Wars:** Anakin is called "Ani," "Padawan," and "Young Skywalker." Later on, he becomes Darth Vader, he is addressed as "Lord Vader," as "My Lord," and he finally returns to being Anakin. The name changes run parallel to the ups and downs of his arc.
>
> **The Matrix:** Neo is addressed as Mr. Anderson, Thomas A. Anderson, and The One. ('Neo' and 'One' are anagrams).[22]
>
> **Harry Potter:** *Harry* doesn't change names too much, which reflects his staying true to his natural humility. The most important symbol for this is when he breaks the Elder Wand: Harry Potter stays (and paradoxically, he *becomes*) Harry Potter.

## Depth by changes in outfit

Clothes (uniforms, insignias, weaponry, accessories, and so on) also reflect changes in status, for better or for worse. Let's review how this works, using once more our example characters:

> **Star Wars:** Little "Ani" is dressed as a slave. Anakin dresses as a Padawan. Darth Vader dresses as the biggest badass in the whole galaxy. Redeemed, Anakin takes off his helmet, telling Luke, *"Just for once, let me look at you with my own eyes."* Note how a gesture that relates to removing a mask symbolizes the return to his authentic self. Finally, "ghostly" Anakin Skywalker is dressed as a Jedi.
>
> **The Matrix:** Neo dresses as an average young guy. Thomas A. Anderson dresses as a corporate employee. "Mr. Anderson" is undressed and humiliated by the Agents. Real-World Neo is dressed as a crewman, almost in rags. The One dresses as the coolest guy ever—sunglasses included.
>
> **Harry Potter:** "Just Harry" (as he identifies himself at the beginning) is dressed almost like a slave. "Mr. Potter" dresses in Hogwarts robes. But then he wears basic clothes:

---

22 - Also, note that "Thomas A. Anderson" is an anagram for "as mother and son," maybe a cryptic foreshadow of Neo having been created by The Matrix. "Matrix," in turn, is a name derived from the word for "cervix," or "mother." Yes, I hereby confirm that I'm a nerd.

Again, this is consistent with a stable arc in terms of status.

A moment in which the outfit is particularly important is when the Hero and the Villain march to the final battle. Examples:

> **Star Wars:** Luke changes into an orange pilot's suit. R2D2 is mounted on Luke's ship, and all fighters are fueled, armed, and ready. In the Death Star, on the other hand, there is no shortage of shiny uniforms, armor, helmets, and insignias.
>
> **The Matrix:** The Agents' suits always look like they were just picked up from the cleaners. Neo and Trinity wear the coolest outfits that anyone can code.
>
> **Harry Potter:** The kids, usually in school robes, are now dressed in street clothes. They aren't students anymore—now they are witches and wizards fighting for their lives.

## Depth by rituals and cycles

I am a fan of nothing. I am a member, supporter, or devotee of nothing.

*No-thing.*

I do some humble and anonymous charity, of course. But I don't belong to any guilds, associations, or fan clubs, and I don't root for any sports teams. I am a citizen of three different countries, but I don't harbor any nationalist or patriotic feelings. In general, I am not proud of (or identify myself) with anything that was given to me, especially not my ethnicity, my surnames, or my nobility titles (of which, incidentally, I have none whatsoever). And in particular, I don't belong to any religious congregations, in spite of my mom's intense advocacy.

However, I totally believe in the need for rituals.

Rituals connect people (fictional and otherwise) to their culture but also to Humankind as a whole. Rituals tell us a lot about a person, too: Does she pray, meditate, or practice yoga? Does she go jogging at 6 a.m.? Does she Netflix-binge? Villains have a "me time," as well. If the story portrays a satanic serial killer, he will need some private ritual, too (which probably will look very different from a Netflix binge).

Rituals have structure, and at risk of forcing too much parallelism, let me say that such structure is similar to the structure of the psyche and, by extension, similar to the structure of stories. See for yourself:

**Rituals follow a script,** which involves particular words, symbols, and actions. Example: swearing on the Bible before giving testimony in a trial.

**Rituals take place intently,** on a select date and time (on the Sabbath, on Sundays, at dawn, at midnight, etc.), obeying to some meaningful reason.

**Rituals are conducted in "sacred" space:** A temple, an open space in nature, a cemetery, a court room, or the privacy of one's room.

**Rituals have a conductor.** If several people take part, they assemble around a center (like in a mandala) in front or around an altar.

**The conductor of the ritual** (judge, priest, etc.) **wears special clothing** and accessories.

**Rituals involve some sensory stimulation**, like incense, music, and chants (as it happens in a catholic mass).

**Cycles,** on the other hand, mark the rhythm of a story, evident in the passing of the hours, of the seasons, and (if relevant to the story's timeline) the passing of years. In a narration without natural time markers, everything feels frozen in time, as if the characters were living inside one of those casinos or shopping malls without any clocks or windows.

Give your characters rituals and cycles. Make them attend a wedding, a birthday party, a Thanksgiving dinner, a sports match, or a funeral, and let them move and react in there. They will feel more real, and the audience may learn a thing or two about them.

# 11. The Key To An Unforgettable Plot

> *"It's a family motto. And I want to share it with you. Here it is: Show me the money. SHOW. ME. THE. MONEEEY!"*
>
> (From *Jerry McGuire,* 1996)

Do you want to know the key to a great plot? Right now? Well, there are many theories, but I will tell you plainly. Pay attention—this is important. Here I go.

## The hook, the glue, and the carrot

Stories need **mystery, intrigue,** and **suspense.** They work differently, and you need the three of them, no matter if it is a detective's or a children's story.

**Mystery is about the past;** it's what hooks the audience: Some unexplained event that happens at the very beginning. *"Wow, what the hell just happened?"*

**Suspense is about the present;** it is the glue that keeps the audience in their seats: Scenes with action and emotion. *"Yikes! And now? What can she do?"*

**Intrigue is about the future.** Intrigue is like a carrot dangling in front of the audience; it's what keeps the reader turning the pages. *"Oh, my God, how is this going to end?"*

Hollywood disagrees with me about that.

Hollywood thinks that it is all about extreme stakes and massive explosions. And so we end up with those adolescent, nightmarish Transformers movies or with eleven shallow superheroes instead of just a really good one.

Hollywood is an industry in which:

> **Mystery is replaced with MacGuffins.** The plot relies too much on an artifact instead of relying on the character's arcs.
>
> **Suspense is replaced with shaky-cam action.** Grown men in spandex tights doing karate chops in front of seven camera operators.
>
> **Intrigue is replaced with exaggerated stakes.** These mega-productions are always about saving the whole Universe. Nothing less will do.

Critic Anthony Lane asked, after watching *Avengers: Infinity War* (2019),[23]

> *"What's wrong with the fate of Hackensack? Doesn't anyone care what happens to South Dakota, or Denmark, or Peru?"*

Indeed, super-productions are always about stakes bloated beyond any credibility, full of aliens coming through space-time portals, looking for an artifact with infinite power that can obliterate the whole galaxy or something.

And many of these bombastic productions are unoriginal to the point of plagiarism. In fact, they are even copying themselves: *Star Wars - The Force Awakens* is an almost frame-by-frame copy of *Star Wars - A New Hope*. I'm not kidding; it's the same movie, with a droid carrying a secret map, a masked villain dressed in black, a Death Star blown up, and even the same lines of dialog. You can watch a side-by-side comparison on YouTube.[24]

Nah, great plots work differently. Oh, if only there were a secret recipe for a great plot!

---

23 - *The New Yorker*, "Avengers: Infinity War" and "Let the Sunshine In" - https://rebrand.ly/01edb

24 - YouTube: Mr. Plinkett's - *The Star Wars Awakens Review* - https://rebrand.ly/4bdfa

## The Secret Recipe for a Great Plot

*What? Do you know the recipe?*

I do, and I will give it to you.

Step-by-step. Right now.

(Please remember this section when you leave an Amazon review for this book, because this is the whole game!)

Here it is:

A great plot is nothing else but **the gradual, suspenseful unfolding of a plan, a plan that is as grandiose as it is malefic.** It is a brilliant, devious, multi-layered scheme, and the Hero must shed a lot of tears while peeling that onion.

Such unfolding complexity can be looked at as a matter of Human Resources because each new revelation relates to higher and higher levels up the dark side's payroll: The audience has to find out who is behind the plan, then who is *really* behind the plan, and then who is *really-really* behind the plan.

In the same way, the audience has to find out about unfolding motives: What is the plot about, what is the plot *really* about, and what is it *really-really* about.

## The structure of an Evil Masterplan

As promised—step-by-step, with an example plot.

**Layer 1: The Hook.**

A bank's manager hires a team of professional hackers and instructs them to rob the bank he works for. *"Hey, why would he do that?"* (Introduces mystery.)

**Layer 2: The public objective** (i.e., what the characters think the plot is about).

What the manager wants is to uncover the weak points of the security system in order to increase the safety of the bank. Or—*wink-wink*—so he says. *(Introduces suspense).*

**Layer 3: The private objective** (i.e., what <u>the audience</u> thinks the plot is about).

The executive wants to rob the bank himself, of course. That's why he is finding out about weak points in the system. (Resolves the initial Hook and kicks the actual plot off).

**Layer 4: The apparent motive** (i.e., what eventually <u>everyone</u> —both the characters and the audience—suspects is the reason behind the villain's plan).

What is he doing this for? For the money, of course. What else would you rob a bank for, right? Or maybe there is something else. (Introduces intrigue.)

**Layer 5: The secret motive.**

Now, why is he *really* doing this? It has to be something deeply personal, something that no one (not the characters, not the readers) saw coming. Remember: The money is just a McGuffin, and the audience doesn't care about MacGuffins—they care about characters.

In this example, what the villain really wants is... Revenge and Recognition, of course! What else? (See Chapter 3)

You see, twenty years ago, this bank financed a corrupt project for the exploitation of a mine in Brazil that collapsed, and the manager's father died in that incident. Now, that incident (the "historical war") should be hinted at the beginning of the story, maybe as some unnamed kid's flashback. *"Hey, who's the kid?"* (Introduces yet more Intrigue.)

**Layer 5: The ultimate motive.**

Check this out: The manager is not even trying to rob the money because, in such a case, the bank would get their money back via the insurance company. What he *really-really* wants is to gain access to the vault and destroy the money right there, sending the corrupt bank to hell. (This is when the hero's Plan-A fails and when the crux of the Villain's plan is discovered. We are 62% into the story here.)

**Layer 6: The moral weakness.**

Up to this point, the villain looks pretty much like a hero. I'm totally rooting for him. But this is where we find a moral fork in the road:

**Path A)** If the manager is an actual villain, the plan needs 1) a moral problem, and 2) a Hero. For example, the money will be destroyed using a powerful C-4 bomb in the middle of the day, killing employees and customers and misleading the authorities into thinking that it was a terrorist attack. The hero could be the leader of the team of experts, who realizes that the bad guy is manipulating them and intends to have them killed in the explosion, too.

**Path B)** If the manager is an Antihero (i.e., a Hero with a dark side), then the story needs a Grand-Villain; for example, the greedy, corrupt owner of the bank, the real responsible for the disaster in the mine in Brazil. The plot could be completed with 1) A slow detective who's always one step behind, explaining to the audience what just happened, and 2) an exciting subplot related to the team of experts, whose leader happens to be the Goddess, who, as we now discover, also lost her dad in the mine explosion, and was working in complicity with the manager from the very beginning.

**Resolution:** Both paths lead to the Evil Twist, and finally, everything will have to be solved with a Virtuous Twist (described below).

Beware of introducing too many layers, though. The story has to stay credible. For example, a way to ruin the story would be: The father of the bank manager didn't actually die in the mine, but it was all a ruse; he changed identities, had facial surgery, and became... The owner of the corrupt bank! Yep, that would be too much, making the audience roll their eyes.

Now, let's talk about the twists. If you are going to remember one line from this book, please let it be this one: **The Evil Twist and the**

**Virtuous Twist is what a story is about.** That's the whole game.

## The Evil Twist

The Evil Twist is a secret element of the villain's plan that nobody saw coming. This ace up the villain's sleeve presents the Hero with the dilemma described back on page 8: No matter what the hero chooses, the unthinkable will happen.

*But when?*

The Evil Twist takes place at a particular moment and only after some specific things have happened beforehand. Like this:

**The Evil Twist happens after** the terrifying power of the dark side has been displayed in full force.

**The Evil Twist happens after** the cavalry has arrived—and failed. The cavalry never resolves the battle; it only allows the Hero to keep fighting.

***The Evil Twist happens exactly*** when the Hero's Plan-B fails.

Also, the Evil Twist triggers The Catastrophe, whatever that means in the context of a particular story. For example, the Hero loses everything, the romance is over, or the giant laser ignited from the alien mothership starts melting New Jersey. The Evil Twist marks the "death" of the Hero and the failure of his quest.

*So, is this The End?*

No, of course not.

## The Virtuous Twist

The Virtuous Twist is like a buzzer-beater—one of those basketball shots in which the ball hits the net after the buzz marks the end of the game. No one saw it coming, either: Not the audience, not the Villain, and not even the Hero himself because his move is not the product of a plan but the consequence of an epiphany. All plans already failed, anyway.

*What's the epiphany about?*

The epiphany is about the Hero realizing the need of an act of self-sacrifice; the epiphany is about finding the courage for transformation.

*The transformation of what?*

Of one into oneself. Stories are an allegory of individuation, so symbolically, this is when the Hero becomes who he really is.

Fundamental: The virtuous twist cannot come out of the blue but must be hinted at along the way. It has to be something surprising but also something that was under the audience's nose the whole time. For example, Harry's epiphany was about realizing that, to kill Voldemort, he must die as well. He clung to the Dark Lord's neck and forced him to jump from Hogwarts' highest tower. *"Come on, Tom. Let's finish this the way we started— together."* Such is the master touch of the Virtuous Twist: The Hero rises through sacrifice, and the inflated ego of the villain spells doom for him. J.K. Rowling accomplished this with just one word: Instead of "Voldemort" or "you a-hole," Harry calls him *"Tom."* Voldemort is forced to see himself once again as the scared little kid who suffered the original narcissistic wound, which puts him out of balance psychologically (and physically, too because down they go.)

*When does the Virtuous Twist happen?*

The Virtuous Twist must happen:

**After the hero has sacrificed it all,** up to his life (or life as he knows it) to defeat the villain.

**As a consequence of the direct use of talent and courage.** The Virtuous Twist must never be a coincidence (a "Deus ex-machina"). No, it must be a matter of destiny, never a matter of luck.

**At the highest moment of the whole story.** This is the climax; this is the moment the entire story has been preparing the audience for.

Let's end this chapter noting that The Virtuous Twist encompasses three stages of the *Ultimate Hero's Journey:*

**The Emergence of the Elixir:**[25] The Hero is brought back from

---

25 - Neal Soloponte, *The Ultimate Hero's Journey* – p. 165

the dead and can continue the battle, this time on a straight path to victory.

Examples:

*Star Wars:* Vader has Luke's ship target-locked; Luke is as good as dead. But the Millennium Falcon is back, shooting everything she's got, and Vader's ship gets kicked out of the sky.

*The Matrix:* Neo is dead. Trinity kisses him, and he comes back to life.

*Harry Potter:* Harry is dead. Hagrid, in tears, carries him. But suddenly, Harry jumps from Hagrid's arms.

**Right Words at the Right Time – part II:**[26] The Mentor is gone, but his words still ricochet in the Hero's mind: He realizes what he has to do. *("Let go, Luke. Trust the Force.")*

**The Apotheosis.**[27] The final battle is over, and the Hero acquires the Ultimate Boon. The Villain either loses, or dies, or is arrested, or is ridiculed. (Or he is left for dead, should you need him for a sequel.) Examples:

*Star Wars:* The Death Star is destroyed in a magnificent explosion.

*The Matrix:* Agent Smith is destroyed in a magnificent explosion.

*Harry Potter:* Voldemort is destroyed in a magnificent explosion.

See? Hollywood loves explosions. I suspect it has something to do with orgasms. Nonetheless, as cathartic as explosions might be, the older I get, the more I prefer poetic endings.

Yep, I'm a romantic at heart.

---

26 - *Neal Soloponte, The Ultimate Hero's Journey – p.170*
27 - *Neal Soloponte, The Ultimate Hero's Journey – p.177*

# Farewell

> *"Gentlemen, you can't fight in here!
> This is the War Room!"*
>
> (From *Dr. Strangelove,* 1964).

**D**irector **Guillermo Del Toro is irritated.** This is what he said about the Hero's Journey:

> *"You have to liberate people from it, not give them a corset in which they have to fit their story, their life, and their emotions. They talk to you about the hero's journey, and you want to f\*cking cut off their d\*ck and stuff it in their mouth."* [28]

Two things come to mind.

One: Every Del Toro movie (every single f\*cking one of them) follows the Hero's Journey down to the last comma. So I don't know what he is so irritated about.

Two: Surprisingly, I kind of agree with what he said.

---

28 - John Yorke, All Stories Are the Same - *The Atlantic* - https://rebrand.ly/e0db0 *(Edited for clarity).*

The very night I finished the first draft of this book, I had what I think was one of the most important dreams of my life.

I sneak inside an abandoned house through a small, broken window. Once inside, I walk through rooms filled with toys: Little model cars, colored cubes with letters and numbers, and a thousand tiny, beautiful things at my reach.

I keep going in, discovering more and more rooms. I explored each one in delight. Soon, I found myself standing in the last room, a bright kitchen with marbled floors, a large stained-glass window full of light, and mahogany panels ornated with bronze acanthus leaves. In the center of this strange kitchen, there was an oak table with many chairs around. This kitchen looked almost like a church—or a mandala.

A man (tall, elegant, and dressed in a black suit) was standing there, looking at me.

*"What are you doing here?"* He said.

I didn't know what to answer, so he spoke again.

*"Well, you finally saw what's down here. Now please leave, and don't come back."*

I woke up.

I know that this was a rare encounter with the Self, the central nucleus of my (yours, everyone's) psyche. And I know what he meant. The message was: "Don't get too fascinated with all this archetype thing. You are stepping into the unconscious—an otherwise inaccessible realm that demands respect."

Remember what Nietzsche said about what happens when you look too long into an abyss?

Now, as it happens at the end of every good story, let's go back to the beginning.

Back in Chapter 1, we wondered: What are good stories about? And I found the answer. I believe that good stories are about healing. Jung, in *'On the Relation of Analytical Psychology to Poetry'* (pars. 129 f.), said,

> He who speaks in primordial images transmutes our personal destiny into the destiny of humankind, evoking the beneficent forces that enabled us to find a refuge from every peril and to outlive the longest night.
>
> That is the secret of great art.

Let that sink in for a minute.

In the meantime, who cares about the Hero's Journey or the opinions of Hollywood celebrities? I say: Let's not obsess too much with this archetype thing. Let's simply join our heroes in their quests, reading (or even writing, if we happen to have it in us) their awesome adventures all the way up to the end.

Because there, after the ink dried into the shape of the final word, we flip through once more, and we find an empty page—a page full of possibilities, an inviting, blank page, shiny like a mirror, one that shows the smiling, true face of the person we are destined to become.

*Se avete mangiato male, ditelo qua,*

*Se avete mangiato bene, ditelo fuori,*

*ma ditelo, cazzo!*


*(If the food was bad, say it here;*

*if the food was good, say it outside;*

*but say it, for f\*ck sake!)*

- Seen in an Italian restaurant in Buenos Aires.

Would you leave a good word for this book on Amazon so other people interested in inspiring stories can find it? Thank you!

Also, if you want to send me an e-mail, you are most welcome: nealsoloponte@gmail.com. I read them all and try my best to answer them all, too.

# Other books by Neal Soloponte

## *What do* **STAR WARS, THE GODFATHER,** *and* **LITTLE RED RIDING HOOD** *have all in common?*

**Not one, not ten, but *195* things!**

Every acclaimed novel and film adheres to a universal narrative structure known as the Hero's Journey. For the first time, with this level of precision, independent writers can delve into Hollywood's blueprint for crafting a classic.

Make no mistake: this isn't just another superficial take on the topic. This is the definitive guide. It outlines all 195 plot milestones present in the most iconic stories ever told, described with clarity and conciseness.

If you're penning a novel or a screenplay, don't start at a disadvantage. Venture into this mythical realm, follow your favorite heroes on **The Ultimate Hero's Journey,** and unravel the quintessential structure of ageless storytelling.

## Other books by Neal Soloponte

**Memories of Another Now** is a novel by Neal Soloponte that aligns its narrative with the corresponding stages from his book **The Ultimate Hero's Journey.**

While you can enjoy this novel as a standalone science-fiction thriller, pairing it with Neal's guide offers a unique insight into the structure of fictional works (see example on the opposing page).

him. I took advantage of his sadness and fury, which destroyed any reservations he had left about kicking some asses of our own. My plan required us to go separate ways, so it was time for goodbyes. And goodbyes suck because you never know if it will be your last.

"I didn't know you could speak Russian," I said.

"My Russian is not that good. I know mostly names of food," he said with a smile, letting me know that he had been on me since the beginning, back in my first meeting with Toby in the CIA basement.

"So, I plug in my card, and your card will find it?" I said.

"They will find each other, no matter the distance."

"Creepy."

Both the night and the rain were falling on the streets of Edinburgh.

Before he left, we fused in a long hug, and then I said, "Don't lose faith. Becoming invisible is my superpower. I'm going to win this."

"You're not invisible to me. And if you think that you can win this alone, you really are mental. In this or any other parallel universe, I'll be there."

"Very creepy," I said, and then, again, we both walked our separate ways.

# Notes

# Notes

# Notes

# Notes

# Notes

# Notes

Made in the USA
Las Vegas, NV
16 February 2025

18247256R00085